The Romans in Britain

The subject of furious   the
National Theatre in Oc   a
three-hour epic play of   ment
fully lives up to its ambi

'If there is one thing t   about a modern play
called *The Romans in Britain*, it is that it will be about
imperialism: in all other respects Howard Brenton keeps us
guessing. Since a large part of his power as a dramatist lies in his
creation of dramatic tension through surprise, it is hardly fair to
reveal all the twists in this complex and fascinating play. But the
central paradox is already contained in the briefest synopsis of
the plot. This is not a play about Roman Britain itself, for
neither of the two parts are set in Roman Britain. The first part
concerns the period before the Roman conquest, the brief and
unimportant second raid by Julius Caesar in 54 BC; while the
second part oscillates between a date a century after the
departure of the Romans (515AD) and the present day. The
play therefore turns out to be about imperialism in a rather
special sense.' Oswyn Murray *Times Literary Supplement*

HOWARD BRENTON
Howard Brenton was born in Portsmouth in 1942 and educated in
Chichester and at St Catherine's College, Cambridge. In 1968 he
joined the Brighton Combination as an actor and writer, and in 1969
he joined David Hare and Tony Bicât in Portable Theatre. His first
full-length play was *Revenge* (1969) which was performed at the Royal
Court Upstairs; this was followed by *Hitler Dances* (1972); *Magnificence*
(1973); *Brassneck* (with David Hare, 1973); *The Churchill Play* (1974);
Weapons of Happiness (winner of the Evening Standard Award, 1976);
Epsom Downs (1977); *Sore Throats* (1979); *The Life of Galileo* (from
Bertolt Brecht, 1980); *The Romans in Britain* (1980); *Thirteenth Night*
(1981); *Danton's Death* (from Büchner, 1982); *The Genius* (1983);
Bloody Poetry (1984); *Desert of Lies* (1984); *Pravda* (with David Hare,
1985); *Greenland* (1988); *Iranian Nights* (with Tariq Ali, 1989). His
four-part thriller *Dead Head* was broadcast by BBC2 in 1986. A novel,
Diving for Pearls was published in 1989.

Also by Howard Brenton

BLOODY POETRY
THE CHURCHILL PLAY
DEAD HEAD
EPSOM DOWNS
THE GENIUS
GREENLAND
HITLER DANCES
MAGNIFICENCE
PLAYS FOR THE POOR THEATRE
REVENGE
THIRTEENTH NIGHT and A SHORT SHARP SHOCK!
WEAPONS OF HAPPINESS

PLAYS: ONE
(Christie in Love; Magnificence; The Churchill Play;
Weapons of Happiness; Epsom Downs; Sore Throats)

PLAYS: TWO
(The Romans in Britain; Thirteenth Night; The Genius;
Greenland; Bloody Poetry)

with David Hare

BRASSNECK
PRAVDA

translated by Howard Brenton

DANTON'S DEATH by Georg Büchner
THE LIFE OF GALILEO by Bertolt Brecht

also available

FILE ON BRENTON compiled by Tony Mitchell

Howard Brenton

THE ROMANS IN BRITAIN

METHUEN DRAMA

First published as a paperback original in 1980 by
Eyre Methuen Ltd.
Second, revised edition 1981
Re-issued in this edition in 1982 by Methuen London Ltd.

Reprinted in 1989 by Methuen Drama,
Michelin House, 81 Fulham Road, London SW3 6RB.

*The photo on the front cover shows Stephen Moore as
Major Thomas Chichester with, from left to right, Peter Harding,
Michael Beint and Michael Thomas as British Soldiers in the
National Theatre Production. Photo by Laurence Burns. The
picture of Howard Brenton on the back cover is by Snoo Wilson.*

Set in IBM 10pt Journal by ⧀ Tek-Art, Croydon, Surrey
Printed in Great Britain by Cox & Wyman Ltd, Reading.

To Jane

The Romans in Britain was first performed on 16 October 1980 in the Olivier auditorium of the National Theatre, London. The play was directed by Michael Bogdanov with settings by Martin Johns, costumes by Stephanie Howard and lighting by Chris Ellis. The cast for both parts is given on pages 10 and 68.

PART ONE

CAESAR'S TOOTH

Nothing human is alien to me
Terence

I have been dead, I have been alive
Taliesin

On the run — A family and its fields — Two worlds touch —
Fugitives and refugees — Caesar's tooth — The gods grow
small — Two murders

The action takes place north of the River Thames on 27th
August, 54BC and the following dawn.

Characters

The cast is as for the National Theatre premiere (see page 6).

CELTS

CONLAG	} *Criminals*	John Normington
DAUI		James Carter
MARBAN	*A Druid*	Greg Hicks
BRAC	} MARBAN's	Michael Fenner
VIRIDIO	} *foster brothers*	Roger Gartland
A MOTHER	*A matriarch*	Yvonne Bryceland
TWO ENVOYS		James Hayes
		Peter Dawson
VILLAGE MEN		Gordon Whiting
		Elliott Cooper
		Peter Needham
		Michael Beint
VILLAGE BOY		Malachi Bogdanov
VILLAGE WOMEN		Susan Williamson
		Anna Carteret
		Terry Diab
		Jane Evers
VILLAGE GIRLS		Loraine Sass
		Chloe Needham

ROMANS

FIRST SOLDIER		Robert Ralph
SECOND SOLDIER		Robert Oates
THIRD SOLDIER		Peter Sproule
GUARD		James Carter
JULIUS CAESAR		Michael Bryant
PREFECT	}	Nigel Bellairs
PRIMUS PILUS	} CAESAR's *staff*	Artro Morris
LEGATE	}	William Sleigh
BUGLER		Colin Rae
STANDARD BEARER		Glenn Williams
ASINUS	*an historian*	Brian Kent
FOURTH SOLDIER		Peter Harding
FIFTH SOLDIER		Peter Dawson
SIXTH SOLDIER		James Hayes
SEVENTH SOLDIER		Melvyn Bedford
SLAVE		Jill Stanford

Scene One

Darkness. Dogs bark in the distance. Silence.

CONLAG. Where the fuck are we?

By the sea?

Daui?

DAUI. Day in, day out. Lying in a boat with salt round the back of my eyeballs. In a river up to my neck. Marshes with leeches. Moors with birds of prey. Rocks with wild cats. In sun, in rain, in snow — I have heard you ask where the fuck are we.

CONLAG. Well.

Where are we?

DAUI. How the fuck do I know?

All I do know is, three days of forest. Then that. Farms. Stockades. Fields.

A silence.

CONLAG. You can smell their food. Smell how their teeth went into it. The little squirts of fat in the meat. The spit that washed it down.

Yeah, you come out of the trees. You smell the meal, the fire, the family. All that you've lost.

DAUI. All that we've shat upon. And has shat upon us.

CONLAG. The criminal life. It's the boils that get you.

Yeah, when you go on the run, you don't think about getting boils.

He sniffs.

Do you smell fish?

They both sniff.

DAUI. No fish.

CONLAG. Could be near the sea, though. Maybe they don't eat fish for religious reasons.

DAUI. Do you hear the sea?

They listen.

CONLAG. Dogs.

DAUI. Dogs.

CONLAG. Dogfish?

DAUI. Just dogs.

CONLAG. Could be a strange sea, this side of Britain. Sea of dogs! Waves of tails! Rabid surf, all froth and teeth! Dogshit beaches!

DAUI. I'd put nothing past this country.

CONLAG. Better get back in the trees. Come dawn, see where we are.

DAUI. Three nights of trees. I'll not sleep under trees again.

CONLAG. Better, Daui. If men make you live like an animal —

DAUI. ⎫
CONLAG. ⎬ Be an animal.

CONLAG. True! It's true!

DAUI. Creepy crawlies. Things that are there and not there. Ghosts. Mantraps. Wild animals. Gods. All that rubbish. I'll not take that again.

CONLAG. But maybe these bastards aren't asleep. Maybe they're fucking. Makes your hearing sharp. Makes you see in the dark too. They'll hear us! Run out and see us! With hard-ons! And kill us — or worse!

A silence. They burst out laughing.

DAUI. I never know when your brain's running out your nose or not.

The sound of DAUI scuttling about.

Not too wet here.

CONLAG. All right, all right. It's wrong. But I'm not the leader of this robber band.

Robber band of two poor fuckers.

DAUI. Brambles here. Do for the sleeper's wall. You got the bag?

CONLAG. Yes I've got the bag.

DAUI. Let me feel it.

CONLAG. I've got the bag.

DAUI. What have you done with the bag?

CONLAG. There is the bag! Dear oh dear.

DAUI. Is it the bag?

CONLAG. What bag do you think it is?

DAUI. You could have changed it for another.

CONLAG. Look —

DAUI. Back in the trees! Someone you're in league with! Some corpse, ghost, thing! That's following us all the time! That you're winking at, behind my back! When people go as low as you, down in the filth like you, I don't know what you do!

CONLAG. You call me low —

DAUI. I don't know what you do!

CONLAG. Feel the iron in the bag. Feel it.

A silence.

DAUI. The wine —

CONLAG. The wineskin's in the bag. Squishy. Feel it.

DAUI's *voice heavy with exhaustion.*

DAUI. Iron and wine.

CONLAG. I'm glad we killed that man we met. And took his iron and his wine. Didn't he squeal! Didn't he squeal!

He laughs.

You sleep first. I'll watch.

DAUI. I could sleep.

But don't drink the wine.

CONLAG. Me? Drink our wine?

DAUI. And don't go talking to yourself. And screaming.

CONLAG. Right.

DAUI. And leave my arse alone.

CONLAG. Right.

DAUI. And don't sell me to 'em.

The things in the trees.

While I'm asleep.

CONLAG *sighs.*

CONLAG. Right.

A silence.

Daui?

A silence.

You don't think — that's what we're going to find?

A silence.

After all our sorrows.

A silence.

And heartbreak. And boils. And my pusy ear. And the thing at the bottom of my spine.

A silence.

Find a dogshit beach?

DAUI. A boat. We'll find a boat. Or people are going to die.

CONLAG. Right.

A silence.

Right.

Scene Two

Dawn comes. An early morning light.

A young woman, a SLAVE, is working at the edge of fields, building a dew pond. She hammers clay with a stone bound to a thick shaft. A stave, a bowl and her day's food in a cloth lie a little way off.

Unseen, CONLAG and DAUI are asleep, hidden by brambles and rags.

The SLAVE looks up and stops working.

CONLAG stands stiffly. He stretches and yawns. He rubs the base of his spine. He turns to find himself facing the SLAVE. Both are still, facing each other.

CONLAG. Don't get the dogs. No dogs. Woof woof. No need for that at all.

Throats. Blood all over the place.

No no.

He kicks the sleeping DAUI.

Daui.

He kicks.

Daui. Get up.

DAUI *comes out of sleep and hiding with a rush, kicking and punching.*

DAUI. Where are they, where are they? I'll kick the shit out of 'em, with my own two hands! What?

The three staring, one to the other.

We're not over your boundary.

CONLAG. Just a couple of Irishmen.

DAUI. No disrespect.

CONLAG. But do not take us lightly! Do not take our powers lightly!

DAUI. We are not on your family's fields!

CONLAG. Travellers in trade. Iron? Wine? So we're protected. Right? Right.

DAUI. If we are on your family's fields, tell us. We'll go. No insult. No trouble.

Nothing from the SLAVE. A silence. DAUI squats, turned away.

CONLAG. What's the name of your family?

The father of your family?

Mother of your family?

Do your fields go to the sea?

DAUI. The thing's a slave.

CONLAG *and the SLAVE stare at each other.*

CONLAG. Yeah?

He nods.

Yeah, I see what you mean.

Eh! Maybe it'll get us food. Even a heavy weapon. Food?

He points in his mouth.

Axe? Eh?

He makes a slicing gesture, smiling widely.

I think they've done that —

He indicates punctured eardrums.

to the ears with it.

DAUI. No. It's foreign.

CONLAG. Kill it?

DAUI. I'm tired. So very, very tired. And they almost got me last night. Things like birds. I couldn't move. I couldn't breathe. I could have sworn they were there. To take my balls out at the roots. In their beaks. And all the rest of me, liver, bowels, soul.

CONLAG. I'm smiling at it — it'll run — get its owners — if we don't do something — like kill it —

DAUI. Obviously. Keep smiling and I'll kill it.

DAUI *pulls the bag towards him and puts a hand in it.*

Three young men in their mid teens run on at the back. They are foster brothers, BRAC, MARBAN *and* VIRIDIO. *They are playing ball. The ball is a sheep's stomach, stuffed with rag and clay.* VIRIDIO *has the ball.*

BRAC. Chuck it!

VIRIDIO. Now! Suddenly he feints.

BRAC. What a wanker.

MARBAN. Hedge him.

BRAC *and* MARBAN *feint around* VIRIDIO *to stop him making a run.*

CONLAG. That's fucked it.

DAUI. Get down!

CONLAG (*to the* SLAVE): You. We're not here. Couple o' ghosts, Gods even, out of the woods, just passing through. Bring you good luck, right? So sh.

DAUI. Get down!

CONLAG and DAUI scramble back into their hiding place.

VIRIDIO digs his heel into the ground.

VIRIDIO. My mark!

BRAC. Never!

VIRIDIO. Count of five! Three four five.

BRAC, a laugh.

BRAC. Piss off.

MARBAN. Make your play, brother.

VIRIDIO. Want me to make my play, brother?

VIRIDIO throws the ball high with a feint to wrong foot his brothers. They run after the ball. BRAC catches it. VIRIDIO and MARBAN tear at his clothing.

BRAC. What's the goal, what's the goal?

VIRIDIO. That hole —

MARBAN. That hole —

BRAC. Oh that hole —

BRAC makes to go one way then goes another.

VIRIDIO. Slippery little arse —

MARBAN. Up in the air!

VIRIDIO and MARBAN run after BRAC, grab him and throw him up in the air.

BRAC. Don't throw me up in the air! You know I hate — (*In the air.*) going up in the air.

BRAC lets go of the ball. They let go of BRAC. MARBAN gets the ball, darts away, stops and calmly puts it on the ground.

VIRIDIO. What's that?

MARBAN. A goal.

VIRIDIO and BRAC stare at him.

BRAC. What goal?

MARBAN. That goal.

MARBAN points at the ball and looks at the SLAVE.

BRAC. I can't see a hole.

VIRIDIO. Hole for the goal, where is it?

MARBAN. It's a small hole.

VIRIDIO. Wormhole.

VIRIDIO laughs.

MARBAN. It is a wormhole.

BRAC, *on all fours, scrambles to the ball. He lifts it carefully and looks underneath.*

BRAC. If you want to find a wormhole, send for a priest.

VIRIDIO. Second sight.

BRAC. Second sight, for seeing the turds of worms.

VIRIDIO grabs the ball and dashes for a few paces.

MARBAN. Brother!

All still.

(*To the* SLAVE:) What is it?

Nothing from the SLAVE. *The brothers look around, sharply. Then* MARBAN *picks up a stone and tosses it to where* CONLAG *and* DAUI *are hiding.*

DAUI *rises, talking fast.*

DAUI. Travellers in trade. From Ireland. Where the fucking heroes come from. But do not take us lightly, do not take our powers lightly.

CONLAG *stands up slowly. A silence, all still.* DAUI *slowly takes an ingot of iron from the bag. A thin bar, about a metre long, the ends pinched.*

Irish iron. To forge, patting butter. Temper it with blood, the phosphorus will dazzle you. And it is very, very hard. Plough with this iron, gold will grow. And a sword? Go through your enemy's gut, a fish through water. And a man's head?

He swings the ingot, two-handed.

His body will stand there, not believing it's his head, bouncing on his big toes. Eh?

A silence.

So could I see the mother or the father of your family?

A silence.

CONLAG. We'll just go now —

VIRIDIO *walks to* DAUI *and takes the ingot from him. He heaves it into the air, it spins, he catches it.*

DAUI. Got loads back there. Cartloads. And all our friends.

Strong, angry, vicious friends.

We just come on ahead. Out of respect.

VIRIDIO. Traders? Sleeping in the open? Hiding from a slave?

CONLAG. Yes, we'll just go now. Take what we've got. There's wine in the bag. Greek wine.

VIRIDIO. Greek wine from Ireland?

The brothers laugh.

CONLAG. We're on our way —

BRAC. Where's this wine, then?

CONLAG *hesitates, then picks up the bag and takes out a wineskin.* BRAC *walks to him, takes the wineskin and drinks.*

CONLAG. Got a load of wine back there. With our friends.
Strong —

He falters.

angry, vicious friends.

BRAC. Greek wine. It's beautiful.

A silence.

Maybe they're Romans.

DAUI. Ha! Ever seen a Roman, farmer boy?

The sun shines out of their navels. Two navels. And big, very big men. In metal. When they walk they clank.

You've never seen a Roman.

MARBAN. Not Romans. (*To* BRAC:) Give me your knife.

BRAC *gives* MARBAN *a knife.*

DAUI. Now don't take that attitude.

MARBAN. They're criminals.

DAUI. Now look, we've not got a disease or anything like that.

MARBAN. Thrown out by their families. Scavenging.

DAUI. Look, we didn't know we were near you, in the dark.

> We'll go on our way. Stay in the woods. Move along the hills. Crawl away from your farms. Not steal your animals.

> You'll not know we've been past!

> *A silence.*

> All right. We're criminals. All right we murdered a man and his wife. All right we were cursed off the land of our families. Our souls taken away by the priests, eh?

> But that was in Ireland. A lot of the world away.

> You've no cause, boys. To put our blood on your fields.

VIRIDIO. Hard luck, Irishman. (*Indicating* MARBAN.) My brother here, is a priest.

> *A silence*, CONLAG *and* DAUI *taking a step back.*

DAUI. I do have a disease.

> *The brothers rush at* DAUI.

> I am a Roman come to fuck your mother —

> *They up-end* DAUI. MARBAN *slits his throat.* CONLAG *runs for it. Blood gushes from* DAUI's *mouth,* VIRIDIO *holding his legs.*

> BRAC, *jumping up and down with excitement.*

BRAC. Wonderful! Wonderful!

VIRIDIO. The other one!

BRAC. We'll get the dogs!

MARBAN. Hold him up! Keep him up!

> MARBAN *looks around.*

BRAC. Get the dogs and go after him, all day, miles and miles!

MARBAN. A stake. (*To the* SLAVE:) You. Your rope and your bowl.

> *The* SLAVE *stays still.*

> Now!

> *The* SLAVE *takes off a rope from round her tunic. She picks up the stave and bowl and holds them out.*

> We'll get him right up! Upside down. Let the blood run into his throat.

MARBAN *runs to the* SLAVE *and takes the rope, stave and bowl. He runs back and digs the end of the stave into the ground.*

(*To* BRAC.) Help, then!

BRAC *helps* MARBAN *to drive the stave in securely.* MARBAN *ties the rope round* DAUI's *ankles and knots the rope round the end of the stave. It bends under the dead weight, the corpse's chest on the ground. He puts the bowl under the neck. This, as* BRAC *speaks.*

BRAC. The little one will go into the woods. We'll run with the dogs. All day. A hot day. We'll shout to him. He'll scream back.

Then, in the afternoon, silence. The woods. He and us. Even the dogs won't bark, just breathe. You'll hear their hearts, thumping.

Brilliant light and dark, under the trees.

And we'll kill him in the evening, and come back home with his head, and get pissed.

VIRIDIO. That done right?

MARBAN. It's not 'Right', but it'll do.

BRAC. Let's go, let's go!

MARBAN. Wait.

MARBAN *takes the bowl carefully from beneath the corpse's neck and tips the blood onto the ground.*

A blessing.

SLAVE (*aside*). They are farmers. They want to put some blood into the cream.

MARBAN. (*to the* SLAVE): Don't let the dogs worry him.

BRAC. Come on, come on.

BRAC, MARBAN *and* VIRIDIO *run towards the woods.*

The MOTHER *comes on. Behind her are the* SECOND VILLAGE MAN *leading dogs and, at a distance, two* ENVOYS.

The three brothers stop before the MOTHER.

MARBAN. Mother!

BRAC. Mother!

VIRIDIO. Mother!
The MOTHER *waves them away. They run off.*

MOTHER. Envoys. You say you are envoys.

FIRST ENVOY. We are envoys.

The MOTHER *stares at the dead* DAUI.

MOTHER. Insults! Nothing but insults, all night long!

SECOND ENVOY. There is a Roman Army —

MOTHER. I offer you dogs as a gift. You want the dogs, you
don't want the dogs. You take the dogs, you insult me. You
don't take the dogs, still you insult me. (*She points at the
sacrifice.*)

And now that! That, another insult!

SECOND ENVOY. What?

FIRST ENVOY. We had nothing to do with that.

MOTHER. You kill people on my family's field? You take
that right away from members of my family?

FIRST ENVOY. Mother of your families —

SECOND ENVOY. Woman —

FIRST ENVOY. With respect —

MOTHER. You booze the night through in my house. You eat
my food. You fight with the men of my family. You eye my
women. You won't take my dogs. You kill strangers.
Outrage!

FIRST ENVOY. All right, we'll take the dogs —

SECOND ENVOY. We are envoys!

MOTHER (*calls out*). Come in from the fields! Take the
children to the house! There has been an outrage!

SECOND ENVOY. Woman! Mother! Cow! Listen!

MOTHER. One of the dogs is a killer. I throw this meat in your
face. Five dogs will lick your hands, the sixth will eat your
lungs!
The FIRST ENVOY *puts a hand on the* SECOND ENVOY's
arm. The FOURTH VILLAGE MAN *runs on and sees the
sacrifice.*

FOURTH VILLAGE MAN. There is blood on the fields.

Shouts, off, in the distance 'Come in from the fields'.

The VILLAGERS *run on, three children with them.*

FIRST VILLAGE WOMAN. Who did it? Did the guests do it?

SECOND VILLAGE WOMAN. Guests — kill on our fields?

BOY. Is there going to be a fight?

GIRL. Are they the men who got drunk?

FIRST WOMAN. Get in the house and shut up. Or you'll get a thump.

SECOND GIRL. But is there going to be fight?

BOY. Can we watch?

FIRST MAN. You heard!

They go off.

MOTHER. Take the dogs. Kill them. They have been insulted.

SECOND ENVOY. We would be very pleased to accept —

MOTHER. Slit their throats! Bury the blood! Throw their bodies in the cess pit!

She throws the meat high, up the back of the stage. The dogs yelp and strain after it.

The SECOND VILLAGE MAN *takes the dogs and runs off with them as the* FIRST VILLAGE WOMAN *and* FIRST VILLAGE MAN *come running back on.*

A silence.

SECOND ENVOY. There is no insult — we killed no-one.

FIRST ENVOY (*low*). Shut up.

A silence, the VILLAGE MEN *and* WOMEN *around the* ENVOYS.

In all decency. Decency. And with dignity. We came as envoys. Spent the night, with your kind hospitality. Ate well.

A night we could not afford. Full bellies we could not afford.

Over the food I said, over the drink I said, again and again.

There is a Roman Army and it is coming.

It is an army of red leather and brass.

It is a ship.

It is a whole thing. It is a monster. It has machines.

It is Roman.

MOTHER. Year in, year out, stories of Romans to scare the children.

SECOND ENVOY. They — are — there!

MOTHER. Eagles instead of heads to scare the boys. Cocks of brass to scare the girls.

The VILLAGERS *laugh.*

SECOND ENVOY. You won't laugh when you're corpses!

FIRST ENVOY. Meat, sizzling in the debris of your burning homes —

SECOND ENVOY. I beg you, woman! You must send the young men and women of your farms. To fight — today.

FIRST ENVOY. Manhood. Womanhood. War. Fury, battle fury. Raise it now.

The MOTHER *spits at the* ENVOYS.

MOTHER. And who sent you?

A silence. All still.

SECOND ENVOY. We have his rings —

MOTHER. You won't say his name.

All night, drinking, singing, arguing, did you.

Even now, you have not got the balls to say the name.

Of the man who sent you.

Not in my house. Not on my fields. Not to my face.

SECOND ENVOY. Cassivellaunel.

A silence.

Cassivell —

The MOTHER *screams. She rocks, one foot to the other.*

FIRST ENVOY. Let us forget old scores, Mother —

She spits.

SECOND ENVOY. What his Grandfather did to your
   Grandfather?

FIRST VILLAGE WOMAN. The cattle raid —

SECOND ENVOY. Five winters back?

FIRST VILLAGE MAN. But never settled.

SECOND ENVOY. Little squabbles.

FIRST VILLAGE MAN. Cattle in winter are not a little
   squabble.

   Laughter.

THIRD VILLAGE MAN. Your Grandfathers were foreigners.

FOURTH VILLAGE MAN. That's right. We don't even foster
   children with you!

SECOND ENVOY. Cassivellaunel was anxious to foster one
   of his daughters with your Mother —

THIRD VILLAGE MAN. And we booted her out —

SECOND VILLAGE WOMAN. No teeth —

FIRST VILLAGE WOMAN. Boil on the end of her nose —

FIRST VILLAGE MAN. Funny smell —

THIRD VILLAGE MAN. Nipples that scratched —

   The VILLAGERS *laugh.*

SECOND ENVOY. You insult our Father's daughter!
   Sons and daughters of a fucking cow, insult our Father's
   daughter!

SECOND VILLAGE WOMAN. Kill the bastards —

FIRST VILLAGE MAN. Ham string 'em, let 'em drag
   'emselves away on their elbows!

MOTHER. Yes yes yes yes! We've had the meal. We've had
   the formal talk. We've had the insults. Yes yes yes!

   A silence.

   So. You want the fighting men and women of the farms
   under my protection to run off south, over the Thames,
   eh?

And the farms left behind? What will they do? Lie here with their legs in the air, fat, fine slobbery pigs, bellies to be ripped open and gorged, eh? With the harvest nearly come? Eh?

While my children, my brothers and my daughters, splash about on the South Coast, hunting Romans that aren't there, eh?

A trick!

Tell Cassivellaunel I still think fondly of his old cock and — tell him to take it in both hands and piss up his arsehole. One pleasantry one insult. He'll know what I mean.

FIRST ENVOY. The Roman Army is there. I have seen it.

THIRD VILLAGE MAN. See your own fart, floating up your nose.

No laughter. A silence.

FIRST ENVOY. The Roman Army moves through this island. A ship of horror. Smashing the woods and farms. Animals run before it. The ship of horror in the water, pushing before it the animals, men, women and children of the farms. Even in this backwater can't you feel it?

They have come from the other side of the World. And they are one. One whole.

Thirty thousand men. Can you, now, see yourself on a beach, the shingle, the tide coming in, and upon it ships with thirty thousand men, eight hundred ships, all one whole? 'Eh? Eh? Eh?' 'Yes? Yes? Yes?'

A silence.

Understand. The Romans are different. They are — (*He gestures, trying to find the word. He fails. He tries again.*) A nation. Nation. What? A great family? No. A people? No. They are one, huge thing.

FIRST VILLAGE WOMAN. He's shit frightened.

SECOND VILLAGE WOMAN. Get away from our farms. Before your blood's on our fields.

FIRST ENVOY. It's an act of truth. What I tell you.

A silence

I have made an act of truth.

The FIRST VILLAGE WOMAN *stoops, picks up a handful of earth and throws it at the* ENVOYS, *not hard, formally. A silence.*

SECOND ENVOY. You won't defend your fields? You —

The FIRST ENVOY *stops him, a hand on his arm.*

FIRST ENVOY. We crossed your boundary, unharmed. We leave it now, unharmed.

The MOTHER *waves them away. The* ENVOYS *take a few steps back, then turn and walk off quickly.*

THIRD VILLAGE MAN. We ought've — whipped their horses into the woods! Sent 'em off with chicken shit down their necks! Let the wild pigs, ride 'em back to Casivellaunel!

FOURTH VILLAGE MAN. We were the hosts, they were the guests —

MOTHER. We can talk about it all day. Or we can work.

FOURTH VILLAGE MAN. The family must be happy Mother. Happy in its mind.

The MOTHER *squats and spits. The* SECOND VILLAGE MAN *comes back on.*

SECOND VILLAGE MAN. I didn't kill the dogs. Didn't want me to, did you?

Nothing from the MOTHER.

Hunting dogs like that.

He looks around the group.

THIRD VILLAGE MAN. If there was an army, there'd be signs. Animals in the woods, running from it. Birds of prey flying towards it, for the flesh. Stragglers, refugees. Listen!

A silence.

Nothing. Just the animals, just our voices, just a day over the farms.

Mother's right. Let's get back to work.

SECOND VILLAGE WOMAN. Though we could, just about harvest now. Dig pits in the woods, hide the crop. (*A short silence.*) It's the time of year for an army, with the harvest almost on us. (*A short silence.*) If there's an army.

FIRST VILLAGE MAN. If pigs fuck sheep!

THIRD VILLAGE MAN. There's no army. Only the old scores.

FIRST VILLAGE WOMAN. But he was frightened. That made me see what he said. I saw his words. The ships on the beach.

FOURTH VILLAGE MAN. A trick of speech. Probably a poet. Powerful men like Cassivellaunel keep a poet or two for that kind of work.

SECOND VILLAGE MAN. We could move the animals to the fort.

A silence. They all look at him, except the MOTHER.

And the old people and children. That at least we could do.

A silence.

FOURTH VILLAGE MAN. That could take four, five days. To get water up there, fuel, the animals of fifty farms. You've not seen it done in your day. I remember the families, barricaded in up there. Just — I was a child. A religious scare. Some druid went off his head and prophesied the end of the world. It caught on and we all ended up in the fort.

We could all get up there. Arm the walls. Miss the good weather — and watch the harvest rot down below.

SECOND VILLAGE MAN. Well, at least consecrate the ground up there.

FOURTH VILLAGE MAN. Oh, we can consecrate the ground.

FIRST VILLAGE WOMAN. And carry weapons in the fields.

A silence.

FOURTH VILLAGE MAN. Mother? (*Nothing from her.*) Consecrate the fort. Carry weapons in the fields. And no drinking during the day. End up cutting ourselves to pieces.

They all look at the MOTHER.

May we leave you?

The MOTHER *waves them away. The* VILLAGERS *straggle off, the* SECOND VILLAGE MAN *hanging back.*

MOTHER. My husband!

The SECOND VILLAGE MAN *turns back.*

You can get *me* a drink.

The SECOND VILLAGE MAN *runs off. The* MOTHER *and the* SLAVE *alone. The* SLAVE *looking at her. The* MOTHER *still squatting, looking down.*

Work, Thing.

The SLAVE *goes back to work. The* SECOND VILLAGE MAN *comes back on with a wineskin. The* MOTHER *pours wine down her throat. She wipes her mouth handing the wineskin to the* SECOND VILLAGE MAN. *He squats and drinks.*

MOTHER. Listen, husband. There is an army.

A silence.

SECOND VILLAGE MAN. You cunning old bitch. You better tell me what you know.

MOTHER. I better tell you nothing.

She drinks. She wipes her mouth.

Tonight, you and my foster sons, dig pits in the woods. Secretly. I want part of the harvest hidden. And go round the fathers and mothers of the farms, the older ones. Get them to do the same. At night. Fast. Before anyone knows what's happening.

SECOND VILLAGE MAN. You'll not keep that quiet. There'll be a row.

MOTHER. If anyone wants a row. I'll row.

SECOND VILLAGE MAN. What do you know!

A silence.

What!

A silence.

You're my wife. Tell me.

A silence.

MOTHER. Two nights ago. The Trinovan families. Sent me an envoy.

They have made an agreement with the Roman Army.

SECOND VILLAGE MAN. Agreement?

MOTHER. They will not fight.

A silence.

SECOND VILLAGE MAN. What do you expect, from fishermen?

MOTHER. The Romans took five hundred hostages, to keep them to it.

SECOND VILLAGE MAN. Five hundred?

A silence

SECOND VILLAGE MAN. What — did you reply to the Trinovan families?

MOTHER. I said that — we foster children with them, not the Cassivellaun families.

That the children bind us.

That their love for the five hundred taken, is our love.

That we are stupid farmers, thick as pigshit.

And we will farm. Just farm.

SECOND VILLAGE MAN. In peace.

MOTHER. Huh.

SECOND VILLAGE MAN. And we — we! Thanks to the treachery of a load of fishermen, we are in alliance with the Roman Army!

None of us have ever seen a Roman!

He turns a circle then stands still.

The forest. The fields. The boundaries. The stockades. The cattle runs. The kilns. The tall roofs of the houses. The Gods on the eaves.

He stamps his foot three times.

The ground in late summer. The thing I know. The thing that's me. The place. Is it changed? Is it —

Is it —

Is it —

Not what I know?

A silence. He reaches for the wineskin. The MOTHER *pulls it away.*

MOTHER. Ah no.

Keep your eyes sharp. And on the chicken. On the pigs. On what's coming out of the trees.

And it'll go by. Whatever it is. Out there.

She stands, walks to the sacrifice, takes the bowl from beneath the dead DAUI's throat and pours blood onto the ground.

Scene Three

River bank and woods. Sunlight. The clothes of BRAC, MARBAN and VIRIDIO on the stage.

A silence. Then the brothers come out of the river, naked and wet. They lie down.

BRAC. In the winter, I'll grow my hair. In the spring I'll dye it. Three colours. Black at the roots, henna, and at the tips, bright yellow.

It will be fucking terrifying.

VIRIDIO. A short arse like you needs to put on a bit of height.

BRAC and VIRIDIO look at each other. BRAC looks away then does a cat leap onto VIRIDIO.

MARBAN lies back with his hands behind his neck, crosses his legs and yawns. Then he suddenly sits up, listening.

BRAC and VIRIDIO stop fighting and look at MARBAN.

MARBAN. I heard him.

A silence.

And the dogs.

A silence.

In the forest.

BRAC. A long way away —

VIRIDIO. Run with the dogs, the short arse said.

VIRIDIO laughs.

BRAC. The dogs will come back, when they've got him. The

leader of the pack will come to tell us. That dog speaks to me. Woof woof, a bone from Ireland. Hero beef.

VIRIDIO. We should've taken the horses.

BRAC. We'd never have followed 'em through the trees.

VIRIDIO. The Iceni ride through the trees. The Iceni can ride into one side of a wood, in chariots, in the shape of an axe-head, and come out the other side, the axe-head still sharp. I saw it done once, at a festival. The forest. The screaming charioteers — disappear.

Silence.

Not even birds rising.

You stare at the wall of trees. Horizon to horizon, a wall of many dark gates.

Then wham! They're coming at you, from anywhere.

BRAC, *playing with his hair.*

BRAC. Great.

MARBAN. A trick.

VIRIDIO. Magic —

MARBAN. It's a trick. They cut tracks through the trees, only known to them. They are silent because the companion of each charioteer muffles the horses' hooves, when they are under cover.

VIRIDIO. Brilliant.

MARBAN. A brilliant trick.

VIRIDIO. Now what would a priest know about tricks?

A short silence. MARBAN, *quietly.*

MARBAN. I'm not a priest yet. And you know it.

VIRIDIO. Ooh!

BRAC. Ooh!

VIRIDIO. He's angry.

BRAC. I think you touched him on his secret rites.

VIRIDIO *and* BRAC *giggle.*

VIRIDIO. Brother is it true, that for part of the training to get to be a priest, you stand for ninety days, with a great big boulder hanging from your testicles?

BRAC *giggles.*

MARBAN. Lie on the ground. A great boulder on your stomach. For ninety days.

A short silence.

VIRIDIO. Well. I s'pose that will come in handy, in later life.

BRAC *giggles.* MARBAN, *quietly.*

MARBAN. Don't be childish, don't be — that. You're my brothers, don't. Eh?

VIRIDIO. Brother, really we are shit scared of you.

(BRAC *giggles.*) I am. Of you.

Because you are going to be a priest. (BRAC *looks embarrassed.*)

MARBAN. Look — no.

If you think — no.

It takes twenty years to be a priest. The thing with the boulder, on your stomach, happens in the ninth year. I've been doing it for three. All right? All right?

Coming home for the harvest.

Though that will stop, in two years' time. And I'll be shut up with them, all the year round.

Huh? Huh?

He looks at BRAC *and* VIRIDIO. *They will not look back.*

They're so happy, those old priests. Those frightening old men and women.

Frightening in the way I begin to frighten you.

Do you want to see a ghost?

A silence.

VIRIDIO. Who am I, a mere wanker in the straw —

MARBAN. No no do you? Now? Right.

MARBAN *goes quickly to his clothes.*

BRAC. Look, eh —

VIRIDIO. Let him.

MARBAN. I go everywhere with her.

VIRIDIO. Her?

MARBAN. It's a woman.

VIRIDIO. Oh good.

MARBAN. Though a ghost.

VIRIDIO. Course.

BRAC. Er —

MARBAN (*at* BRAC). Someone dead. Beyond the grave. Not in our world.

MARBAN *takes a flint stone with a hollow ground in it. He puts a powder in the hollow. He takes another flint stone, flaked to a point to fit the hollow in the first stone. He takes a length of cloth and wraps it round his fist as he gives his patter.*

Have you thought why, since we all live beyond the grave, in the sweet fields, the rich woods there — we don't see them more often, the dead?

BRAC. Well —

MARBAN. Because of the pain of dying, brother.

Which is like a wall.

BRAC. Ah.

MARBAN. Solid, thick with pain.

So the cracks in the wall of death are rare. Tiny.

And the life of the dead can only flare through them, for a moment.

As they do, in the lights over a marsh.

Like this.

MARBAN *hits the two flintstones together. A muffled report. A cloud of white smoke drifts up and away.*

VIRIDIO. That was a woman?

BRAC. I saw her —

VIRIDIO. What was it?

BRAC. Lovely thighs —

MARBAN, *unwinding the cloth from his hand.*

VIRIDIO. A trick?

BRAC. Like silver.

MARBAN. A ghost a trick, a trick a ghost.

If the religious shit themselves, what's the difference?

Huh? Huh?

He laughs.

VIRIDIO. They do say 'Never look a priest in the eyes.'

BRAC. Like a dog! Send the dog mad —

VIRIDIO. Which one is the dog though, looker or priest? Eh?

VIRIDIO and BRAC stare at each other.

BRAC. Yes but —

VIRIDIO and MARBAN staring at each other.

Look, don't.

A silence.

Don't.

A silence.

Start fucking insulting each other next.

MARBAN (*to* VIRIDIO). I've been taught an insult.

Which, if it's made to you, your eyes melt. Your tongue, tears itself out. Your head — bursts.

It's only a few words.

Want me to say it?

To you?

They stare on. Then VIRIDIO *looks down.* MARBAN *giggles.*

VIRIDIO. Now he's taking the piss.

BRAC. Stories about priests, getting up each other in the woods. My father always hated 'em. Rant and rage, 'bout how the richer families send off their favorite sons to join 'em. How their visions, auguries, judgments of disputes, were always — in your favour if — (*A turning gesture with his hand.*) A fine animal or two, fine iron, fine wine —
Then, round they'd come. And my poor old father — he'd go religious quicker than a billy goat fucks.

VIRIDIO *looks away, then does a cat leap onto* MARBAN. They laugh and fight.

MARBAN. Get off.

VIRIDIO. What, brother —

MARBAN. Get off —

VIRIDIO. Dear oh dear.

VIRIDIO *rolls away. The three brothers lie in the sun.*

Still. It's hot. The water was good and cold.

The dogs are tearing down an enemy, somewhere in the woods.

Along with the wild pigs, and your priests, in there, doing what they do.

Where's the Irishmen's wine?

BRAC *hands* VIRIDIO *the wineskin. He raises it to drink.*

Three ROMAN SOLDIERS *walk out of the woods. The soldiers and the brothers see each other at the same time. There is a considerable distance between them.*

A silence.

FIRST SOLDIER. Three wogs.

A silence.

SECOND SOLDIER. What are they, d'you know?

THIRD SOLDIER. A wog is a wog.

FIRST SOLDIER. Not Trinovante. Not round here.

THIRD SOLDIER. Pretty arses. Give 'em something.

The SOLDIERS *laugh.*

VIRIDIO. They — not got eagles on their shoulders 'stead of heads. We'll see in a moment if they've got brass balls that clang when they walk.

VIRIDIO *laughs.*

MARBAN. Be quiet.

VIRIDIO. They don't know what we're saying. We don't know what they're saying.

BRAC. Kill the leader first. Which one's the leader? Can you tell which one's the leader?

MARBAN. Shut up! (*Low:*) What weapons have we got?

BRAC. My knife —

MARBAN. Where?

BRAC. You had it. To cut the Irishman's throat —

MARBAN. Yes.

A silence.

One knife. Under my clothes — don't look at it!

Stand up.

The brothers stand.

FIRST SOLDIER. A little wander round, and we pick a plum. Not that we don't deserve it. Fine day? Sun? A swim? Three little wogs to play with?

SECOND SOLDIER. There may be others. (*He looks around.*) I mean these are children. Maybe they sent 'em out to play, while they're hiding, waiting to come down on us.

THIRD SOLDIER. No, these wogs are fucked and do they know it. Success is with us, the news of success — right? So — wade right through 'em, into the river, right?

BRAC. Jabber jabber.

MARBAN. They're talking about how to kill us.

VIRIDIO. They're between us and the trees.

MARBAN. We've got one knife.

We don't know who is best to use it.

BRAC. Me —

VIRIDIO. Me —

BRAC. With a knife? Oooh!

BRAC, a knifing gesture.

MARBAN. Be still!

A silence.

Get them to circle round. Then we can get into the trees.

The SOLDIERS *advance toward the brothers carefully.*

SECOND SOLDIER. Don't let 'em get into the trees. I've seen enough of wogs running into the fucking trees.

THIRD SOLDIER. Beads? Pretty beads?

FIRST SOLDIER. For fucksake.

The FIRST SOLDIER *draws his sword.*

Italian short sword, eh? Want to feel your fist round that? A real hard-on, eh?

He spins the sword in the air. MARBAN *takes a step back. The* SOLDIERS *stand still.*

A silence.

The SECOND *and* THIRD SOLDIERS *draw their swords.*

The SOLDIERS *run at the brothers.* MARBAN *runs to his clothes and gets the knife.* VIRIDIO *and* BRAC *run in different directions.*

The SECOND *and* THIRD SOLDIERS *catch* BRAC *and give him a bad stomach wound.*

BRAC *rests, pulls himself along the ground, screams, rests — a progress that continues during most of the rest of the scene, gradually slowing.*

VIRIDIO *stops, turns and stares at his brother's agony.* MARBAN, *with the knife, turns.*

All but for the crawling BRAC *are still.*

VIRIDIO. Foreigners, I will hold your heads in my hands. With my fingers in the sockets of your eyes, I will hold up your skulls, wet with the flesh of your eyes and your blood! I will know you as a killer! As only the killer can know the thing he has killed! To hold you, the guts of you, the kidneys and the hearts of you in my fists! And you will smile, when your heads are dry bone! Over my house! My children and my grandchildren will play with your skulls! And I will tell of the meal we will have tonight! Of you! Of your brain, turned over a fire! With your guts fed to the pigs! Your arseholes gnawed by my dogs! I will hold your bloody hearts, today! Today! Up to the sun as it sets, and squeeze, and your blood will run down my throat, and I will drink you, get pissed on you! And vomit on you and drink more of you! You will be blood in my bones! You will feed me, my meat, my enemy! And your mothers, wherever those stinking sows lie, in your stinking country, will wake with a cry in their own shit, and tear their tits with the pain of how I am going to kill you!

FIRST SOLDIER. Jabber jabber.

SECOND SOLDIER. Keep the one with the knife off.

The FIRST SOLDIER walks toward MARBAN and feints him away from the SECOND and THIRD SOLDIERS, who, with their shields, calmly crowd in on VIRIDIO, slam their shields against him and kill him. They step back.

VIRIDIO slides to the ground with a wound in his chest and in his back.

THIRD SOLDIER. What a waste of pretty arse.

A silence.

The three SOLDIERS and MARBAN — four young men standing still.

Then, relaxed, the SOLDIERS walk to surround MARBAN, each a good way from him.

With the knife ready MARBAN turns from one to the other. Then he relaxes.

A silence, but for BRAC.

FIRST SOLDIER. I'm just here for a swim.

SECOND SOLDIER. That (*Meaning BRAC.*) may be heard.

THIRD SOLDIER. That (*Meaning MARBAN.*) would've yelled, if there were more.

FIRST SOLDIER. I'm going to get that swim, so let's —

The FIRST SOLDIER runs at MARBAN. MARBAN side steps and slashes the knife at the FIRST SOLDIER, catching his arm. Surprised, the FIRST SOLDIER falls, turning with a reflex out of his training to cover himself with his shield.

Fucking little nig nog.

He staggers to his feet.

He cut me!

The SECOND SOLDIER laughs.

THIRD SOLDIER. What are we waiting for?

The SOLDIERS run at MARBAN, smashing their shields against him from three sides. MARBAN's knife goes flying, he stumbles away and falls. The FIRST and THIRD SOLDIERS begin to strip.

Hold him, then.

SECOND SOLDIER. I'll do him in the neck.

THIRD SOLDIER. Don't , he'll shit himself.

FIRST SOLDIER. All this trouble for a bit of a swim.

THIRD SOLDIER. No, I want him to feel this. You can cut him about a bit if you want. Here!

The THIRD SOLDIER *picks up* MARBAN's *knife and tosses it toward the* SECOND SOLDIER.

Use his knife.

SECOND SOLDIER. I wonder about you sometimes.

THIRD SOLDIER. Cut him! Make him look pretty!

SECOND SOLDIER. Dear oh dear.

The SECOND SOLDIER *picks up the knife and makes a cut on* MARBAN's *shoulder blade.*

THIRD SOLDIER. Got no fucking idea at all, have you.

The THIRD SOLDIER, *now half naked, takes the knife from the* SECOND SOLDIER, *kneels and cuts* MARBAN *on the buttocks.*

MARBAN *moans, as if with a question, looking at the* SECOND SOLDIER *who holds him by the shoulders.*

MARBAN. Hunh?

The SECOND SOLDIER, *into* MARBAN's *face.*

SECOND SOLDIER. My friend has been to the Orient. Persia? Funny little ways he's picked up, in his career. But what the fuck do you expect, from a man who's been in Persia?

MARBAN. Hunh?

SECOND SOLDIER. Hunh?

THIRD SOLDIER. Ooh, he's begun to shit himself.

SECOND SOLDIER. Persia? The other side of the world?

MARBAN. Hunh?

SECOND SOLDIER. World?

MARBAN. Hunh?

THIRD SOLDIER. Rub it in. Make it smooth.

SECOND SOLDIER. Empire?

MARBAN. Hunh?

The FIRST SOLDIER *is now naked. He spits on his cut arm and rubs the spit in. The* THIRD SOLDIER *holds* MARBAN's *thighs and attempts to bugger him.*

FIRST SOLDIER. Just a scratch.

SECOND SOLDIER (*to the* FIRST SOLDIER). You pig.

He laughs.

THIRD SOLDIER (*to the* SECOND SOLDIER). Y'can — y'can give us a kiss.

SECOND SOLDIER. Fucking Greek.

THIRD SOLDIER. Yeah.

FIRST SOLDIER (*examining his belly*). I've got little spots. I'm coming out in little spots.

THIRD SOLDIER. Go — and have — a swim — you're taking my mind — off what I'm doing.

FIRST SOLDIER. I will.

The FIRST SOLDIER *cartwheels.*

THIRD SOLDIER. Keep this fucking arse still!

SECOND SOLDIER. Sorry, veteran of Persia.

The SECOND SOLDIER *blows the* THIRD SOLDIER *a kiss.*

FIRST SOLDIER (*cartwheeling*). Days and days — I have wanted a swim.

He cartwheels off, into the river, out of sight.

THIRD SOLDIER. This in't no — in't no — at all —

SECOND SOLDIER. In trouble, comrade?

THIRD SOLDIER. In't no arse at all.

The THIRD SOLDIER *rolls away.* MARBAN *begins to struggle.*

MARBAN. Hunh hunh hunh —

THIRD SOLDIER. Not even got it up anymore!

MARBAN. Hunh hunh —

The SECOND SOLDIER *hits* MARBAN *on the top of the head with the butt of his sword.* MARBAN *is knocked unconscious. His left leg twitches twice then is still.*

A silence.

THIRD SOLDIER. Oh. (*He sits up.*) Oh oh.

SECOND SOLDIER. I said, are you in trouble comrade?

THIRD SOLDIER. Arseful of piles. Like fucking a fistful of marbles. I mean, what do they do in this island, sit with their bums in puddles of mud all year long?

He stands.

Huh.

He looks at himself.

And I'm covered in shit.

The SECOND SHOULDER, *running his hand over* MARBAN's *back.*

SECOND SOLDIER. Good shoulders.

THIRD SOLDIER. I don't want you talking about this.

SECOND SOLDIER. Did I say a word?

THIRD SOLDIER. I don't want to hear a word.

SECOND SOLDIER. If that's your attitude.

THIRD SOLDIER. Marcus Clavius. I do not want to hear, one night out drinking, back home, years from now, on a lovely evening, surrounded by admirers, sons. I do not want to hear — of me not getting it up a British arseful of piles. Right?

SECOND SOLDIER. Right.

THIRD SOLDIER. I know how rumours start.

SECOND SOLDIER. Right.

THIRD SOLDIER. I mean. (*A half laugh.*) Pride. And it's been a fuck of a summer.

SECOND SOLDIER. Go and have a swim. (*They look at each other.*) Wash yourself off.

THIRD SOLDIER. I will. (*He backs away.*) Right.

He runs into a handstand. He jack-knifes out of it. He turns and looks at the SECOND SOLDIER.

Good.

*He goes to the riverbank and dives in, out of sight. The
SECOND SOLDIER runs his hand over MARBAN's back
again, under his shoulder, scrutinizing his finger's path, over
the temple and into MARBAN's hair.*

BRAC is now still and silent.

SECOND SOLDIER. Soft bone, where I hit you.

My uncle, a slave, he was a slave, was hit there.

He spits. He rubs saliva into MARBAN's hair.

When he was a man of some years. Thirty. And he couldn't
speak. Couldn't —

*A gesture at his mouth. He puts his finger back into
MARBAN's hair and runs it round to his mouth.*

My uncle was treated kindly, by his master, he began to get
words back. Gave him his freedom, out of kindness. Now he's
with the priests of a cult, oracle, holy oracle. You've got a
lump of phlegm in your mouth.

He turns MARBAN's head on its side.

Halfway up your nose, here — bloody too, if you're bleeding
into the back of your nose you'll choke on that — here.

He pulls out the mucus and wipes his hand on the ground.

There. Choke on that. I saved your life, nig nog. A legionary
saved your life, nig nog. Nephew of a slave. Now, a citizen,
upon my discharge.

(*Running his finger round MARBAN's mouth.*) If I don't get
gangrene, eh? And get off this fucking island, eh? My discharge,
upon a little bit of bronze — 'Citizen'.

He breathes out and looks up.

Come on come on.

He leans over MARBAN and kisses him.

Get you over. Come on.

He turns MARBAN over with difficulty. MARBAN comes to.

MARBAN. Sacerdos sum. Exsecrationem scio. Te miles romane,
caedet. Foede!

SECOND SOLDIER. A nig nog? Talking Latin?

MARBAN *gags. The* FIRST *and* THIRD SOLDIERS *come out of the river, wet. The* SECOND SOLDIER *straddles* MARBAN, *knees beside his head.*

This nig nog talks Latin!

THIRD SOLDIER. What do you think you're doing? (*He laughs.*)

SECOND SOLDIER. He talks Latin!

THIRD SOLDIER. Watch it. He may bite off more than you want him to chew. (*He laughs.*)

SECOND SOLDIER. Fucking Latin talking nig nog! Suck me off!

FIRST SOLDIER (*looking at his stomach*). Those spots. They've gone violet.

Scene Four

Deep woodland. Pools of darkness, shafts of sunlight.

CONLAG *is killing a dog, pulling its back legs over its back, rolling, trying to keep the dog from biting him.*

CONLAG. Leader! Leader are you! Leader of the pack are you! 'Ere. (*Winning.*) 'Ere, 'ere. (*Laying over the twitching dog.*) There. There.

He stands, holding the dog by its back legs. He screams at the surrounding forest, turning.

All right dogs! Here's your leader! Fucker of your wives! Eat him now! I'll get out your way now! Up a tree, over a stream!

Eh? Take — (*Whirling around, swinging the dog with two hands.*) him!

He throws the dead dog. It falls on the ground. He runs a few paces then trips and falls.

Oh I've hurt my foot, oh!

He lies still. A silence. He looks behind him.

No dogs?

He jerks himself into a crouch.

I just killed the lead dog of a pack and they're not chewing my balls? Pack of fucking British hunting dogs?

What else they gone off for? What's rawer than me? Juicier?
(*He giggles.*) Something that's died! And I am still alive. I.
Am. Oh my foot.

He sits back from his crouch and looks at his foot.

If your feet go in times like these, you may as well bury
yourself. Right there. Up to the waist. Some warrior band or
another will be along to cut you to peices.

(*He stands.*) It's all right! (*He falls.*) It's not all right. (*He
shouts.*) It's got to be all right!

(*He stands. Low:*) Oh fuck.

He walks a few yards with difficulty.

The SLAVE, *startled in a hiding place, stands up. They stare
at each other. A silence.*

I threw a dead dog away, somewhere round here. Something
to eat, in the days ahead. Eh?

A silence.

Burn the farms, did they? Run off, did you?

He laughs. She steps back.

I'm not after your hole. I've been in and out of it all. That's
nothing to me. Help me to walk. (*She stays still.*)

I'm a murderer. (*She stays still.*)

I've got a bad foot. (*She stays still.*)

Me and Daui. We were going to the sea. Get a boat. Now he's
dead. So you come with me.

She stays still.

There is a land. The stories say it's there so it's got to be. Over
the sea. The forests are thick. The deer are free. The pigs are
there for the taking. Put your hand in a river there, the fish
come to kiss your fingers. And no Gods, no creepy crawlies,
no souls of dead heroes bashing around in the undergrowth,
giving you the shits. And no people! No people! It is there!
The stories say so!

Off we go then.

*They are both suddenly startled. They stare in the same
direction.*

Something —

She gestures 'Be quiet.' A silence. They hear it again.

Your owners, running. Or Romans running after them.

He laughs. The SLAVE slaps his face. He stares at her. She pulls him down into hiding.

The two VILLAGE WOMEN and the FIRST, THIRD and FOURTH VILLAGE MEN with the three CHILDREN come on, quickly, in a bunch. The THIRD VILLAGE MAN is wounded.

FIRST GIRL. Were they Romans?

SECOND GIRL. They didn't have eagles instead of heads.

BOY. Why did they burn us?

SECOND GIRL. Are we going to kill them?

BOY. Why did they burn us?

FIRST GIRL. *Are* we going to kill them?

FIRST VILLAGE WOMAN. Shut up, children!

She gestures to the group. They crouch down, still.

A silence.

A considerable space between the two groups.

FOURTH VILLAGE MAN. Something.

A silence.

SECOND VILLAGE WOMAN. Nothing.

FIRST VILLAGE MAN. I had a sling in my hand. I turned. The house was burning. I ran toward the house. Behind me, the field burst into flames. My daughter ran toward me. Burning. She fell, fire between us. I stood in the smoke. Then I was an animal. Running, to get in the trees. In the dark.

He vomits.

THIRD VILLAGE MAN. Humiliation.

SECOND VILLAGE WOMAN. Catapults. On little machines. Throwing burning —

FOURTH VILLAGE MAN (*to the* THIRD VILLAGE MAN). How bad are you —

SECOND VILLAGE WOMAN. Just like that. From nowhere.

Throwing burning —

FIRST VILLAGE WOMAN. Get to the sanctuary. Leave the children with the priests. Find the families.

THIRD VILLAGE MAN. Hit back. Again and again.

FOURTH VILLAGE MAN. Let me look at you —

The THIRD VILLAGE MAN *pulls himself away.*

FIRST VILLAGE MAN. I didn't even see 'em! Not one of 'em! Just a great ball of fire, rolling over the crops toward me. Then in me.

FOURTH VILLAGE MAN (*to the* FIRST VILLAGE WOMAN, *shaking his head*). Bad.

THIRD VILLAGE MAN. We must get a Roman's head. Carry it alive. In a little bag. On the end of a stick. So it can cry out in terror to its countrymen. And its screams will be clean, clean, clean as a knife, to cut out our humiliation —

FIRST VILLAGE WOMAN. Be quiet!

A silence. They look around. The sound of their breathing.

CONLAG. Crawl away from this lot, girl. They'll be cutting themselves and everything that moves to bits.

The SLAVE *helps him up. They move a few steps. They freeze. The* VILLAGERS *have heard them.*

FIRST VILLAGE MAN. Tracking us. Circle 'em. Stick the pigs.

FIRST VILLAGE WOMAN. Shut up.

A silence.

FOURTH VILLAGE MAN. Only our kind can move as quiet as that.

A silence.

Let them go. Who knows whom we can trust now?

The two groups steal away from each other.

Scene Five

River bank and woods. The bodies of BRAC *and* VIRIDIO *on the ground.*

Upstage a group of ROMAN SOLDIERS *stand very still — a* STANDARD BEARER, *holding a legion standard, two fully armed* SOLDIERS *and a* BUGLER.

A silence.

Two SOLDIERS, *in tunics, run on with a stretcher, on it the bodies of the* MOTHER *and the* SECOND VILLAGE MAN, *her husband. The* SOLDIERS *tip the bodies onto the ground and run off with the stretcher.*

A silence.

A punishment squad of three SOLDIERS, *in tunics, and a* GUARD *come on. They are laden with piles of wooden lavatory seats and spades.*

GUARD. Field lavatory detail!

FIRST SOLDIER. All right all right we're behind you.

SECOND SOLDIER. I am sick of digging lavatories.

GUARD. Then don't end up in a punishment squad.

THIRD SOLDIER. Something to tell your kiddies, when you get back home.

SECOND SOLDIER. Oh yeah. I dug a shit hole on the edge of the world.

They throw the seats down in a heap.

GUARD. A good fathom down, lads.

They begin to dig.

JULIUS CAESAR *wanders forward from the back looking at the ground. He is followed at a distance, though closely observed, by members of his staff —* ASINUS, *a historian in civilian clothes, a legionary* LEGATE, *a legionary* PREFECT, *and a* PRIMUS PILUS — *a centurion of the highest rank, a man in his early sixties.*

CAESAR *stops. His staff stops. The punishment squad stop working and stare.*

A silence, all still.

CAESAR *stoops and picks up* MARBAN's *knife. He walks on. The punishment squad return to work.*

Dangling the knife casually at his side between finger and thumb CAESAR *walks by the* MOTHER's *body, ignoring it.*

CAESAR. Prefect of the Legion.

The PREFECT *runs forward.*

Set the standards.

PREFECT. Yes General.

CAESAR. Don't pitch camp yet. Wait for the order.

PREFECT. Yes General.

CAESAR. Be careful with their bodies. Consecrate the ground. Set up an altar.

PREFECT. General.

The PREFECT *goes back to the staff.*

CAESAR. My bugler.

The BUGLER *runs forward.*

Let them know I'm here.

BUGLER. Yes General.

PREFECT (*to the* PRIMUS PILUS). Set the standards. The order to pitch camp has *not* been given.

PRIMUS PILUS. Yes Sir. (*He shouts*:) First Standard Bearer!

The STANDARD BEARER *runs forward. The* BUGLER *blows a call.*

A runner down the lines. The order is set the standards. Wait for the bugle to pitch camp.

STANDARD BEARER. Yes Sir.

The STANDARD BEARER *digs his standard into the ground, then begins to run off. The* SOLDIERS *take up guard of the standard.*

CAESAR. Wait.

PRIMUS PILUS. Stop where you are.

The STANDARD BEARER *stops.*

LEGATE. Gaius Julius Caesar. This is my command. It is my privelege to receive your orders —

CAESAR (*ignoring the* LEGATE). Primus Pilus. (*The* PRIMUS PILUS *runs to* CAESAR. *Privately*:) What did we do here?

PRIMUS PILUS. A couple of cohorts got jumbled up in the trees. The runners lost contact. Then they came on this lot —

CAESAR. And had some fun.

PRIMUS PILUS. Without orders, one thing led to another. (*Carefully*:) What with —

CAESAR. What with an invasion that's deteriorated into a squalid little raid, eh Centurion?

Nothing from the PRIMUS PILUS.

I'm not angry with the men. Let that out, down the lines.

PRIMUS PILUS. General.

CAESAR. Stay. (*Calls out*:) Prefect. (*The* PREFECT *runs to* CAESAR.) Any sign of them regrouping?

PREFECT. Nothing. We came on them suddenly and dispersed them.

CAESAR. Prisoners?

PREFECT. Some.

CAESAR. Dead?

PREFECT. No Romans. Of them — (*He shrugs.*)

CAESAR. Think they're getting together in the trees, Centurion?

PRIMUS. What wogs do in the trees, General —

CAESAR. Quite. I want to give the men a rest. What do you think?

The PREFECT *and the* PRIMUS PILUS *uncertain.*

Quite. (*A silence.*)

Divided watch. An hour's recreation for the men stood down. Then change round. No alcohol. For every man swimming a man in battle readiness, watching the trees.

PREFECT. Yes General.

CAESAR *waves them away.*

(*To the* PRIMUS PILUS:) That order down the lines.

PRIMUS PILUS. Sir.

The PRIMUS PILUS *walks quickly to the* STANDARD BEARER. *They talk privately for a few moments, then the* STANDARD BEARER *runs off.*

The LEGATE, *near tears, walks towards* CAESAR.

LEGATE. This is my command. You are humiliating me, before the Legion —

CAESAR *walks away.*

CAESAR. Asinus, my friend.

ASINUS *walks to* CAESAR, *who leads him away from the* LEGATE.

What tribe was it we've just cut to pieces?

ASINUS. As far as I can see, not Trinovante. But a loose grouping, a handful of families —

CAESAR. In the federation of the Trinovantes?

ASINUS. Probably sympathizers.

CAESAR. Sympathizers of sympathizers with us.

ASINUS. Yes.

CAESAR. Wonderful. Is their chieftan killed, or what?

ASINUS. The body of a woman was bitterly fought over. That body.

He points to the body of the MOTHER. CAESAR *doesn't look.*

CAESAR. A woman?

ASINUS. They are not belgaic, they do not originate from the mainland. They are of the ancient stock of Britain. Traces of matriarchy are to be found among them. The Iceni —

CAESAR. All right all right! (*A silence.*) Forgive me. Your scholarship is invaluable. But I've got toothache.

ASINUS. I'll call a surgeon —

CAESAR. No no. (*He calls out:*) The Legate of this legion. (*The* LEGATE *comes forward quickly.*) (*To* ASINUS:) Stand back. But overhear us. Conspicuously.

ASINUS *steps back. A silence.*

LEGATE. Protector of my family —

CAESAR (*angrily*): You what?

A silence. Then CAESAR *holds the knife up by its tip, looking at the handle.*

See, I would like to know how they lay the bronze into the iron. Curling patterns. Like marketry, but with metal. Very fine and on a simple hand weapon. I could have you stoned by your own soldiers for what happened here. (*A silence.*)

Stoned. (*A silence.*) Do these niggers have steel? The Celts of Northern Italy had steel, eh?

(*Over the* LEGATE's *shoulder:*) Asinus, when we come to a smithy, look to see if there are steel tools.

The LEGATE *looks at* ASINUS *and back to* CAESAR.

Or did they just trade it from abroad, eh? For a dog, eh?

CAESAR *tosses the knife and catches it by the handle.*

I am not the protector of your family, Aurelius Drusius. I just seduced your sister.

LEGATE. I know you are angry with me, I learn from your anger, it is justified, I —

CAESAR. Don't. (*A silence.*) Don't begin to speak like that. Don't go down that path. Ten sentences and you will be promising to kill yourself. Then you will have to kill yourself. And you will never forgive me. Nor will your family.

LEGATE. I speak from the heart.

CAESAR. A disgusting, fashionable habit.

LEGATE. I have no cynicism —

CAESAR. Nor have I! (*He stares at the* LEGATE.) I take rhetoric very, very seriously. In war, what is done is done. In speech, what is meant is meant. You're a young man, learn how a Roman must speak. Of his life, in public, at moments like this. When you are being reprimanded, for having lost control of your command, during a minor mopping up exercise, against a wretched bunch of wog farmers, women and children, in a filthy backwater of humanity, somewhere near the edge of the world.

A silence.

There. I've spoken of your tiny stupidity — and ended with the world. Textbook rhetoric, little to big? Eh? (*He grimaces, tonguing his bad tooth. He massages his face. He stops.*)

A silence.

It's an affliction.

A silence. He sniggers.

I think I am going to make a remark for the Official Biography, Asinus.

ASINUS, *notes at the ready.* CAESAR *sniggers again.*

I was going to say it's an affliction, to see in any one act, its consequence. To see a man — (*He gestures at the* LEGATE.) and see his future. At once. Bang, like that.

In any predicament, its opposite. To build a tower, knowing brick by brick, how it can be destroyed. Even in the victory of an enemy, I see his defeat.

Once I was captured by pirates. Island fishermen really. I told them — when my ransom is paid, I will return and kill you.

My ransom was paid. I raised a fleet. I stormed their islands. I crucified them all, all their communities, twenty thousand of them, men women and children! Wooded islands. The crosses took all the trees. The islands will be rock and turf for ever. A logic. I walked in forests as a captive. Free, the same ground had to be a barren plain. One extreme the mother of the opposite extreme.

After all, my ancestral mother is Venus, Goddess of love, and I am a man of war.

He sniggers. A silence.

LEGATE. What —

CAESAR. What's your future? You — (*He puts his arm round the* LEGATE's *shoulders.*) will die, a little before me, a very old man, very rich, very happy and very senile. You are relieved of your command in all but name and show. The Prefect of your legion will take his orders directly from me. You will stay on my staff. Your humiliation as a military man will be politely obscured. If you protest, you will be stoned by your soldiers, with relish. The political consequences of maltreating so favourite a son would be tiresome, but easily overcome by my party.

LEGATE. I —

CAESAR. No no no. Put it like this, are you my friend, or aren't you, eh? (*Hugging the* LEGATE.) What d'you say?

LEGATE. I'm your friend.

CAESAR. What a fucking island, eh? What a wretched bunch of wogs, eh? Go and have a swim.

LEGATE. Yes, General.

CAESAR. Look, send this knife to your sister, as a present from me. Tell her — (*He toys with the knife.*) to guard with this knife, what I would enter as a knife.

LEGATE. I —

CAESAR gives the knife to the LEGATE.

CAESAR. She reads Terence, she'll understand. (CAESAR *takes the knife back.*) I'll have it cleaned up. A box made. Maybe a human pelt to wrap it in, eh?

LEGATE. Thank you, Gaius Julius.

The LEGATE *hesitates, then walks away and off the stage.* CAESAR *watches him for a while then turns away.*

CAESAR. The politics of the Roman dinner table are with us, even on the filthy marshes of the edge of the world, eh Asinus?

ASINUS. Yes.

CAESAR. I want him killed. An auxiliary, pissed. A slave with the grievance. Anything — (*An angry gesture.*) trivial. Arrange it.

ASINUS. Yes. Do you want to see something odd?

CAESAR. Odd?

ASINUS makes a sign. Two SOLDIERS *come on with* MARBAN, *still naked, bound.* CAESAR *looks at him.*

Well?

ASINUS. This Celt talks Latin.

CAESAR (*to* MARBAN). Do you? (*Nothing from* MARBAN.) Soldier, go and cut the head off the body of that woman.

The SOLDIER *moves.*

MARBAN. No!

CAESAR stills the SOLDIER *with a sign.*

CAESAR. Why not?

Because then I would own her soul?

MARBAN (*low*). Fitness of things.

CAESAR. What?

SOLDIER. Speak up to the General rubbish!

MARBAN. It would be against the fitness of things!

A silence.

CAESAR. How clumsy your obscene superstitions sound in my language, Druid.

Which is what you are. No?

Nothing from MARBAN.

SOLDIER. Speak up rubbish!

CAESAR (*to the* SOLDIER). No no. (*To* ASINUS:) We know Druids on the mainland speak Greek. Even write it. It's no surprise to find a little Druid in Britain, talking Latin.

ASINUS. All the tools of civilisation. And they keep their people in ignorance.

CAESAR. Hunh. Let him go.

The SOLDIERS *push* MARBAN *forward. He stands, still bound, shivering.* CAESAR, *with disgust.*

Look at the way they live.

A silence.

I'm going to let you run back into the woods, little Druid.

CAESAR takes a pendant from his neck.

Tie that round his neck. Tight.

The SOLDIER *does so,* MARBAN *writhing.*

Let him go in the woods. Still bound. His fellow priests will find Venus around his neck. (*Suddenly fierce.*) Listen listen to me! On the mainland I burn your temples. Your priests that will not serve the Roman Gods — I kill. I desecrate their bodies. Desecration according to your beliefs. The head off and burnt, etcetera. Because there are new Gods now. Do you understand? The old Gods are dead.

Nothing from MARBAN.

Yes, you understand. We are both religious men. (*To the* SOLDIERS:) Give him fifty lashes before you let him go. To make the point.

SOLDIER. Yes General.

CAESAR waves them away. The SOLDIERS *take* MARBAN *off.*

CAESAR. What did we come to this island for, Asinus?

ASINUS. Fresh water pearls —

CAESAR. So we did. Leave me.

ASINUS. Gaius Julius.

> ASINUS *walks away then, at a discreet distance, turns and watches* CAESAR.

CAESAR. Primus Pilus. You and two men.

PRIMUS PILUS (*to the* SOLDIERS *guarding the standard*). You and you.

> *They go to* CAESAR.

CAESAR. Stand with your backs to me.

PRIMUS PILUS. General.

> *The* PRIMUS PILUS *nods to the* SOLDIERS. *They stand with their backs to* CAESAR. CAESAR *stoops forward, feeling his tooth with his fingers. Then he holds his lips back and loosens the tooth with the point of the knife. The punishment squad stop work and look.*

FIRST SOLDIER. What is our General doing?

SECOND SOLDIER. The moody sod wants to be alone.

THIRD SOLDIER. Sometimes a man has got to be alone. (*They laugh.*)

GUARD. Get on get on.

> *With a grunt* CAESAR *pulls his tooth out. Blood on his fingers. He looks at the tooth.*

ASINUS (*aside*). He is a man waiting on the edge of the world. For what? In a sense, he does nothing. He only reacts. And finds himself master of continents. It is not surprising that he pays historians to find omens of great things at the time of his birth.

> CAESAR *throws his tooth away.*

CAESAR. Vinegar.

> *The* PRIMUS PILUS *gives* CAESAR *a flat bottle. He sluices his mouth out and spits.*

> *Stones begin to fly over the stage, landing amongst the Romans.*

FIRST SOLDIER (*this is, of the* SOLDIERS *guarding* CAESAR).
Wogs. Throwing stones.

SECOND SOLDIER. Slings.

PRIMUS. General —

CAESAR. Yes. Quickly.

SOLDIERS *running, shields over their heads. The* SOLDIERS
guarding CAESAR *hold their shields* above him.

PRIMUS PILUS. Bugler! Standard Bearer!

CAESAR. Prefect of the legion.

The STANDARD BEARER *and* BUGLER *run to the*
PRIMUS PILUS. *The* PREFECT *runs to* CAESAR.

PRIMUS PILUS. Men out of the water. First and second
centuries of the fourth cohort, up to the trees with missiles —
they are not, *not* to enter the forest. Bugler, defensive
formations.

The BUGLER *blows a call. The* STANDARD BEARER *runs
off.*

CAESAR. Yes?

PREFECT. Can only be a handful. With slings. Even children.
Dying down now.

CAESAR. We will not pitch camp. We go south, now.

PREFECT. General. Primus Pilus!

PRIMUS PILUS. Sir.

PREFECT. Strike the standards.

PRIMUS. Sir. Bugler! Marching order!

The BUGLER *makes another call.*

CAESAR. Asinus, record this order.

ASINUS. Yes General.

CAESAR (*to the* PREFECT). Take their animals. Salt the fields.
Kill the prisoners. Do what you can in the time.

PREFECT. Yes General. Primus Pilus, with me.

They hurry away.

CAESAR (*to* ASINUS). Even a little massacre must look like
policy. They'll take it as a warning. Or that we knew these

people were traitors. Probably leave a little local war behind us — no bad thing.

(*To the* SOLDIERS *shielding him:*) Join your squads.

The SOLDIERS *run off.* CAESAR *walks away upstage, followed by* ASINUS.

The SOLDIERS *of the punishment squad.*

FIRST SOLDIER. Not making camp? What about our lavatories?

GUARD. Leave 'em for the Britons. Teach 'em an healthy habit.

SECOND SOLDIER. I am always digging lavatories on this campaign which are never used.

GUARD. That's the speed of modern warfare.

Scene Six

Moonlight. The fields.

MARBAN *is sitting on the ground, legs skewed beneath him, still naked and bound, the Venus pendant round his neck.*

A silence.

The FIRST *and* SECOND VILLAGE WOMEN *and* FIRST, THIRD *and* FOURTH VILLAGE MEN *come on. They have weapons at the ready, and dart about searching, stopping, listening, looking.*

Then they are all still.

A silence.

FIRST VILLAGE MAN. They've gone. (*A silence.*) Into the ground?

SECOND VILLAGE WOMAN. There.

She points to MARBAN. *The* FIRST VILLAGE MAN *approaches him cautiously.*

FIRST VILLAGE MAN. Where are your brothers?

FOURTH VILLAGE MAN. Salt! Salt on the fields! (*He weeps.*) They'll put salt on the fields.

FIRST VILLAGE MAN. Where is our Mother?

FOURTH VILLAGE MAN. They've poisoned us.

FIRST VILLAGE MAN. Your brothers and your mother —

THIRD VILLAGE MAN (*nursing his wound*). Maybe they're defeated. Maybe —it's peace.

FOURTH VILLAGE MAN. Maybe they tortured him, put him here as a decoy, ambush, while we weep with him for our fields —

THIRD VILLAGE MAN. No. It's peace.

FOURTH VILLAGE MAN. And poison.

FIRST VILLAGE MAN. Boy —

SECOND VILLAGE WOMAN. He's tied up. Cut him free.

The FIRST VILLAGE MAN *hesitates.*

Go on!

The FIRST VILLAGE MAN *cuts* MARBAN *free and steps away quickly.*

At once MARBAN *tugs at the Venus round his neck, gets it off and throws it away.*

MARBAN. Give me a knife.

A silence.

When they let me go I stayed in the trees, near them.

I knew I was — filthy! Filthy! Defiled! With one of their Gods round my neck! Give me a knife!

FIRST VILLAGE WOMAN (*quietly, to the* FIRST VILLAGE MAN). Don't.

A silence.

MARBAN. They're marching to the coast. To cross to the mainland. Give me a knife.

A silence.

FOURTH VILLAGE MAN. Gone.

MARBAN. No.

THIRD VILLAGE MAN. Defeated?

MARBAN. No.

THIRD VILLAGE MAN. But —

They look at each other. A silence.

FIRST VILLAGE WOMAN. Make clearings in the forest, before the cold weather. New fields, hidden —

SECOND VILLAGE WOMAN. Get through the winter, to plant them —

FIRST VILLAGE WOMAN. We'll see in the morning, how much they've burnt —

MARBAN. Give me a knife! (*He laughs.*) I am a priest. A seer. I see. (*He laughs.*)

Three years, the salt will drain out of the fields. And in the fourth year? Will you dare creep out of the hidden fields in the forests, to plant another harvest? To watch the nightmare of another raid, ripening through the year?

Oh the life of the farms will go on.

But you'll never dig out the fear they've struck in you. With their strange, foreign weapons.

Generation after generation, cataracts of terror in the eyes of your children. And in the eyes of husband for wife and wife for husband, hatred of the suffering that is bound to come again.

They've struck a spring in the ground beneath your feet, it will never stop, it will flood everything. The filthy water of Roman ways.

He laughs.

They'll even take away death as you know it. No sweet fields, rich woods beyond the grave. You'll go to a Roman under-world of torture, a black river, rocks of fire.

We must have nothing to do with them. Nothing.

Abandon the life we know.

Change ourselves into animals. The cat. No, an animal not yet heard of. Deadly, watching, ready in the forest. Something not human.

FIRST VILLAGE MAN. And live off what, priest?

MARBAN. Visions. Visions. Stones. Visions. (*A silence. Then, dead voiced:*) The ghosts of our ancestors, slink away. The fabulous beasts, their claws crumble. The Gods grow small as flies.

He weeps quietly.

FIRST VILLAGE WOMAN. Give him a knife.

The THIRD VILLAGE MAN *puts a knife before* MARBAN.
*He looks up from weeping, at the knife. He holds it upwards
in his fist, on the ground, his arm extended. He raises himself
up and is falling on the knife —*

Scene Seven

Dawn. The north bank of the River Thames.

CONLAG *and the* SLAVE *are wandering downstage, she helping
him to hop along. He is feverish.*

CONLAG. The sea!

SLAVE (*aside*). It's not.

CONLAG. The beach!

SLAVE (*aside*). It's the River Thames.

CONLAG. The shingle's slippery.

SLAVE (*aside*). It's mud.

CONLAG. Don't get the dogshit on my bad foot! In a day, in a
    night, how can a foot puff up, right up to your groin? It's not
    fair! It's not right! After all I've been through! There's a
    boat.

SLAVE (*aside*). It's a log.

CONLAG. Sh. Fishermen.

SLAVE (*aside*). Branches on the log.

CONLAG. Down down down down.

They fall in a heap. He crawls over her, toward the 'log'.

I'll kill them.

SLAVE (*aside*). He did rape me in the forest.

CONLAG *and the* SLAVE *pick up stones at the same moment.*

CONLAG. Pick up a stone. Sharp edge. Cut off their heads. Blood
    on the sea. A holy road, over the waves.

The SLAVE *walks to the crawling* CONLAG *and hits him on
the back of the neck with her stone. He grunts, then turns
over on his back and looks up at her. She stands there
relaxed, the stone in her hand.*

You can be my wife, in the forests, in that land. The animals are so tame, you just kill them for food. They'll not learn fear of men and women. For generations.

She raises the stone high above her head and brings it down hard on CONLAG's *forehead. He dies at once.*

SLAVE (*aside*). On the island where I was born. Over the sea. Where he wanted to go. Only stone. Nets for the fish. The tomb, where my mother was buried, along with all the others. The children saw the ship first, with a sail with an animal on it. We were clever with stones. All the children. Wherever I am it's not left me. When they kept me in a pit. When they fucked me in the forest. When they made me work in a field. I always knew what stones were near me. How many steps to them. Count one, two — and what stone would be in my hand. The men from the ship burnt my home. Now home is where I have a stone in my hand.

In the distance, the sound of an approaching helicopter.

From the back the Roman Army advances in British Army uniforms and with the equipment of the late 1970's.

First a patrol of five soldiers, four privates and a CORPORAL. *The* SLAVE *looks at them.*

FIRST SOLDIER. There's one of 'em.

SECOND SOLDIER. Drop that, or I will have to open fire!

The SLAVE, *still.*

SECOND SOLDIER. Drop that, or I will have to open fire!

THIRD SOLDIER (*into a two way radio*). Charlie Bravo, we have a contact.

The SLAVE *throws the stone at the* SECOND SOLDIER. *and hits him in the face. The* FOURTH SOLDIER *opens fire with his automatic weapon, the* SLAVE *is blown back by the impact, dead.*

CORPORAL.   } What the fuck do you think you're doing!
FOURTH SOLDIER. } Chucked it right in his throat!

FIRST SOLDIER. Jack!

THIRD SOLDIER } (*into the radio*). Charlie Bravo we have a casualty.
CORPORAL.   } Look! Look for more of 'em!

All but the FOURTH SOLDIER *crouching, covering the area. He runs at the* SLAVE's *body and kicks it.*

FOURTH SOLDIER. Fucking bogshitting mick!

CORPORAL. All right all right!

FOURTH SOLDIER. In his throat!

CAESAR and his staff, in the dress of British Army Officers have driven on in a jeep and are getting out.

CORPORAL. All right!

The FOURTH SOLDIER *kicks the* SLAVE's *body again.*

FOURTH SOLDIER. Kick the shit out of your fucking country!

CORPORAL. Shut up lad!

CAESAR. What's that?

PREFECT. A contact, Sir.

FOURTH SOLDIER. Sending little girls out against us now.

CORPORAL. All right.

The noise of the helicopter is louder now.

FOURTH SOLDIER. Sorry.

CORPORAL. Yeah yeah. Just walk away lad and have a good spit. (*To the other* SOLDIERS:) Come on! See if that's wired. Then roll it into the water.

The SOLDIERS *inspect the* SLAVE's *body.*

PRIMUS PILUS. The 'copter will have to hover Sir, too risky to land —

CAESAR. Yes thank you. (*Aside.*) That everyday life will begin again. That violence will be reduced to an acceptable level. That Civilisation may not sink, its great battle lost.

CAESAR and the staff turn away.

CORPORAL. Anything on her?

FIRST SOLDIER. Just stones.

The helicopter roaring.

PART TWO

ARTHUR'S GRAVE

The world's enigma: Arthur's grave.
The stanzas of the graves

A blunder — An old man and his fields — A soliloquy — The dead Saxon — The contact — The last Roman Lady — An execution — The making of Arthur.

The action takes place in Britain in 515 AD and in Ireland in 1980 AD.

Characters

The cast is as for the National Theatre premiere (see page 6).

MODERN TIMES

THOMAS CHICHESTER	Stephen Moore
CORPORAL	Michael Beint
BRITISH SOLDIERS	Robert Ralph
	Robert Oates
	Peter Sproule
	Peter Harding
	Peter Dawson
	Melvyn Bedford
BOB MAITLAND	William Sleigh
IRISH WOMAN	Yvonne Bryceland
O'ROURKE	James Hayes
IRISH MEN	Greg Hicks
	Michael Fenner
	Roger Gartland

515AD

PRIEST		Brian Kent
CAI		Gordon Whiting
VILLAGERS		Elliott Cooper
		Glen Williams
		Nigel Bellairs
SAXON SOLDIER		Melvyn Bedford
MORGANA ⎱	*CAI's*	Terry Diab
CORDA ⎰	*daughters*	Anna Carteret
ADONA	*A Roman Matron*	Susan Williamson
FIRST COOK ⎱		John Normington
SECOND COOK ⎰	*ADONA's*	James Carter
STEWARD ⎰	*servants*	Peter Needham

Scene One

A field, harvested, the corn in sheaves. Dawn light. THOMAS CHICHESTER, in farm worker's clothes, walks about the field. He smokes.

CHICHESTER. Dawn. Waiting. Near the Irish border.

Who are you talking to? You Tom. Right Tom? Dawn near the Irish border.

He turns a full circle on his heel, scanning the countryside.

Who are you waiting for, Tom?

A man called O'Rourke.

Come on, Sheamus Naill O'Rourke.

He is startled. He crouches down. He looks about him nervously. He takes out a drinking flask.

Got the hoojahs, Tom. Because of the field. Four pine trees. The dead likeness of the Old Acre. A field back home, on the family farm.

Could see my mother — coming out of the trees now. Telling me to get my hair cut — that I'm drinking too much.

And where is home, Tom?

England, Tom.

Four pine trees. Traces of banks.

Hard men can weep for home, Tom.

Shut up.

Yes shut up you bloody idiot.

He is about to take another swig of the flask when a whistle blows. British Army SOLDIERS come into the field at the back through the trees.

No! No!

CHICHESTER *scrambles into a hollow, trying to hide.*

You bastards.

CORPORAL. We go from this field. Right down through the woods, to the track.

CHICHESTER (*to himself*). No. No, no, no, no.

CORPORAL. And anything. Anything. A fucking blade of grass pointing the wrong way — you call an NCO.

FIRST SOLDIER. Our Corporal is jumpy this morning.

The two SOLDIERS *near him laugh.*

SECOND SOLDIER. Your first time on the border, in't it lad?

THIRD SOLDIER. You don't know yet.

FIRST SOLDIER. Know what?

THIRD SOLDIER. Look at it. Little fields, little hedges. Hills in the pale blue yonder. Pretty, in't it?

FIRST SOLDIER (*shrugs*). Yeah.

THIRD SOLDIER. Could be anywhere. Well it's not. 'Cos you are a Brit and a Squadie and to you what you are walking on is the surface of the moon — and very, very dangerous.

FIRST SOLDIER. Still. Nice day for it.

SECOND SOLDIER. Oh dear oh dear, a little hero.

THIRD SOLDIER. We're moon men. We should have space suits, oxygen, the lot.

FIRST SOLDIER. I joined the Army 'cos I liked canoeing.

SECOND SOLDIER. Oh we all joined the Army 'cos we liked something.

CORPORAL (*walking past them into the trees*). Stop talking over there!

Two SOLDIERS, *downstage, see* CHICHESTER.

FOURTH SOLDIER. Corporal!

All the SOLDIERS *in the field stop. The* FOURTH *and* FIFTH SOLDIERS *cover* CHICHESTER *with their guns. The other* SOLDIERS *are dead still.*

FIFTH SOLDIER. Do not move or I will have to open fire!

CHICHESTER. Piss off.

The FIRST SOLDIER *raises a whistle and blows it. The* CORPORAL *comes running out of the trees.*

CORPORAL. Oh my God.

As he runs he takes out a pistol. He reaches the FOURTH *and* FIFTH SOLDIERS.

(*To* CHICHESTER:) Get up on your feet, slowly.

CHICHESTER. Why does the British Army have to be so bloody British? Brains like boots. Balls like King Edward potatoes. Thick as pigshit.

FIFTH SOLDIER. Shut up!

CORPORAL. Stand up slowly. Put your hands behind your head. If you do not we will have to open fire.

CHICHESTER (*does so, speaking in Bertie Wooster*). Don't twist your knickers, Corporal. I'm touring Ireland for my hols. To have a look at the Celtic crosses and the Guinness.

FOURTH SOLDIER. He does — ah — sound British, Corporal.

CORPORAL. Are you? British?

CHICHESTER (*in immaculate Belfast*). I take that badly, coming from a British Soldier. Who's walking all over my country, like he did God Almighty's job and made it.

FIFTH SOLDIER. Sounds fucking West Belfast to me —

CORPORAL. Shut up. (*To* CHICHESTER:) Right. Who are you, where do you live and what is your business here?

CHICHESTER (*in immaculate Dublin*). I am the Bishop of Dublin. Smuggling the sacred relic of St Patrick's foreskin, over the border for Ian Paisley to suck on.

FOURTH SOLDIER. He's a joker. (*He laughs.*)

CORPORAL. I'm sick of fucking jokers in this country. Search him —

CHICHESTER. Stay where you are!

They hesitate at CHICHESTER's *tone.*

Get me an officer. Now.

CORPORAL. Search the bugger!

FIFTH SOLDIER. Down! On your face! Hands behind your back!

CHICHESTER *makes a kiss to the* FIRST SOLDIER, *who hits him in his stomach.* CHICHESTER *doubles up and goes down.*

CHICHESTER. Not — clever — get an officer —

FOURTH SOLDIER. Shut up!

The SECOND SOLDIER *kicks* CHICHESTER *who rolls to protect himself.*

CHICHESTER. You silly buggers — (*He laughs.*)

FIFTH SOLDIER. Want more do you, Bishop —

CORPORAL. Just search him. (*To the other* SOLDIERS:) And you lot. I want every little Irish worm in this field shitting up his little worm hole.

CHICHESTER (*weeping*). Mummy! Mummy! Mummy! Can I have a British Army Soldier to play with at Christmas?

He laughs. Beyond himself, the FIFTH SOLDIER *pulls* CHICHESTER's *head up by the hair.*

FIFTH SOLDIER. Shut up! Shut up!

CORPORAL. Stop that!

FIFTH SOLDIER. He is annoying me!

CHICHESTER (*calmly*). Just tell an officer to pop along old chap.

CORPORAL. I said let go his hair!

The FIFTH SOLDIER *does so.*

Go over him, carefully. (*To the other* SOLDIERS:) All of you! Be careful! Keep your eyes open! (*Into a two-way radio:*) Red Bravo. Red Bravo. We have a suspect.

The FOURTH SOLDIER *finds a pistol in* CHICHESTER's *clothes.*

FOURTH SOLDIER. A pistol, Corporal.

CORPORAL. Oh yes? (*The* CORPORAL *takes it.*) Czechoslovakian

CHICHESTER. Funny little souvenirs a tourist picks up in Ireland.

FIFTH SOLDIER. Be quiet!

FOURTH SOLDIER. Drink on his breath. And not breakfast time yet —

The FOURTH SOLDIER *hands the* CORPORAL *the hip flask.*

CORPORAL. This kind of thing makes me nervous. Why isn't anything straight in this fucking country?

LIEUTENANT BOB MAITLAND, *walks down from the back of the field quickly.*

MAITLAND. What is it, Corporal?

CORPORAL. A suspect, Sir. Armed.

He gives MAITLAND *the pistol.*

MAITLAND. Czechoslovakian.

CHICHESTER. Is that an officer?

FIFTH SOLDIER. Keep your face on the ground.

The CORPORAL *hands* MAITLAND *the flask.*

CORPORAL. And this Sir. He's half-cut Sir.

CHICHESTER. Nothing but the real thing. Irish booze and iron curtain gun.

MAITLAND. Stand him up.

CHICHESTER *is hauled to his feet. He and* MAITLAND *stare at each other.*

Oh no.

CHICHESTER. Keep your mouth shut.

MAITLAND. What the hell are you doing here —

CHICHESTER. Shut up!

A silence.

MAITLAND. All right, Corporal. I'll talk to this johnny.

CORPORAL. Yes Sir. You two!

The CORPORAL *leads the* FOURTH *and* FIFTH SOLDIERS *away.*

CHICHESTER. Don't let them chuck the sheaves about. I harvested this field with my own bare hands.

MAITLAND *stares at* CHICHESTER, *then turns to the* CORPORAL.

MAITLAND. Corporal. Do it neatly.

CORPORAL. Neatly. Yes Sir.

FOURTH SOLDIER. What's all that about?

CORPORAL. We don't see, we don't hear.

FIFTH SOLDIER. Sometimes I think we're just in Ireland to dig toilets.

CORPORAL. Enough. (*To all the* SOLDIERS:) Come on lads! The Pope is hiding somewhere in this field. Give his holiness a big surprise.

MAITLAND. Sorry if they pushed you about.

CHICHESTER. Don't worry old man. I have had special training to deal with pain. Pain is not the problem.

MAITLAND. You do owe me an explanation. Am I going to get it?

CHICHESTER. Bobby, Bobby Maitland. What a prick you are, Bobby.

How are all the other chums in my old Regiment?

MAITLAND. Oh the Regiment's in good fettle.

CHICHESTER. 'Good fettle.' Ha! With their tanks on the Rhine. Short of brains and spare parts —

MAITLAND. I am trying to keep my temper!

CHICHESTER. I am trying to keep my life!

Three months I've been setting up an operation here. Building respect. There's an old woman up in the farmhouse — don't bother her.

MAITLAND. All right all right —

CHICHESTER. I work the farm for her. Her sons are in the Kilburn High Road — or the Costa del Sol.

MAITLAND. How do you, of all people, pass yourself off as Irish?

CHICHESTER. Oh I sing a few rebel songs in the local pub.

MAITLAND. Tom, are you following orders? Or are you off on some madcap scheme of your own?

A silence.

Tom —

CHICHESTER. I am doing my bit to win the war in Ireland. Now you and the Queen's baboons in Army boots are putting my operation here in jeopardy, so piss off.

MAITLAND. I have to ask you again. Are you following orders?

CHICHESTER. A kind of order.

MAITLAND. What does that mean?

CHICHESTER. A sense — of the order — of things.

MAITLAND. What are you talking about?

CHICHESTER. It's a Celtic idea. Pagan.

MAITLAND. Not gone native, have you?

CHICHESTER. Ha!

It's Celts we're fighting in Ireland. We won't get anywhere 'til we know what that means.

Look at this field. It's like one on my mother's farm, not far from Colchester. The Roman city of Camulodunum.

One Spring, ploughing, we found a God. That big. Celtic, pagan. And Camulodunum could be the site for Arthur's last battle. AD515.

King Arthur! Celtic warlord. Who fought twelve great battles against the Saxons. That is, us.

MAITLAND. What are you talking about?

CHICHESTER. The Celts! Ha! Very fashionable, the Celts, with the arty-crafty. Ley-lines. Druids. But show them the real thing — an Irishman with a gun, or under a blanket in an H-block and they run a mile.

If King Arthur walked out of those trees, now — know what he'd look like to us? One more fucking mick.

MAITLAND. You're a maverick, Tom Chichester. And a romantic and a bloody menace. God! I joined the Army for tanks. Where are my tanks? On the banks of the River Rhine. Where am I? Poking about on foot, in an Irish field.

This may be some kind of crusade for you. But for me — Irish, Celt, they're all murdering bastards.

CHICHESTER. Look, old regimental chum. I out-rank you.

MAITLAND. I thought that was coming. Sir. (*Offering the pistol and the whisky flask.*) You want these back?

CHICHESTER. Not in full view!

MAITLAND. There's no sign —

CHICHESTER. They're here. They're always here. This is their bloody country. If they saw you take them off me — you've done for me, old chum. Give me the whisky and drop the gun in the straw.

MAITLAND *does so.*

Now get me that Corporal.

MAITLAND. Corporal!

CORPORAL. Sir! (*He approaches.*)

CHICHESTER. Corporal. Why are Catholic tarts the best?

CORPORAL. Er —

MAITLAND. Answer Corporal. This is an officer.

CHICHESTER. Because they've got rhythm. Sir.

Corporal!

CORPORAL. Sir?

CHICHESTER. Who was the hardest man who worked on the M1 Motorway?

CORPORAL. An Irishman who got his cock stuck in the cement, Sir!

CHICHESTER. And Corporal —

CORPORAL. Sir?

A short silence.

CHICHESTER. What does careless talk cost?

CORPORAL. Lives, Sir!

CHICHESTER. Your balls for sure. Tell every man in this field that.

CORPORAL. Sir.

CHICHESTER. Now hit me again.

CORPORAL. Sir?

CHICHESTER. I am an Irish labourer in a field, who gave you some lip.

So hit me hard.

MAITLAND. Do it.

The CORPORAL *hits* CHICHESTER *in the stomach.*
CHICHESTER *doubles up.*

CHICHESTER. (*shouts in Northern Irish*): Hey, Soldier. You know what your Queen is? A cunt wrapped up in a Union Jack.

The CORPORAL *kicks* CHICHESTER, *angrily.*

MAITLAND. All right thank you Corporal!

CORPORAL. Sir!

MAITLAND. Pack up here.

CORPORAL. Sir. (*To the* SOLDIERS:) All right. That's it. Back to the transport. (*He moves away.*)

MAITLAND. You're probably a brave man. But I think you're off your head.

CHICHESTER. That may get me the first Victoria Cross in Ireland.

MAITLAND. Only if we declare war.

CHICHESTER. Quite. Now stop endangering my life and limb and get out of here. Right away.

MAITLAND. Right —

CHICHESTER. Bob, if I get bumped off ask my mother to throw my ashes on the Old Acre field.

MAITLAND. I —

CHICHESTER. My mother is a stern old cow. Insist.

MAITLAND. Are you serious?

CHICHESTER. Fuck off.

MAITLAND. Yes. Goodbye.

CHICHESTER. Toodle-oo.

MAITLAND *walks away quickly. The* SOLDIERS *go off at the back.*

CHICHESTER, *alone. He sits. He covers his face with his hands. Then he drinks from the flask and lies down, curled up.*

He stays on the stage as —

Scene Two

515AD. A long silence. CAI, an old man, walks into the field. He is followed at a good distance by a PRIEST and three VILLAGE MEN: The VILLAGE MEN carry the bundles of refugees. The PRIEST carrys a staff with a cross at its top. CAI squats.

PRIEST. Saxon soldiers, Cai. Coming North, over the Thames.

FIRST VILLAGER. They've been seen!

SECOND VILLAGER. A mile from the village!

PRIEST. At least think of your daughters.

CAI. Bah. (*CAI spits.*)

THIRD VILLAGER. They may be here, in your field — in the heart of Britain. Today!

PRIEST. We leave under Christ's cross. Carrying what we can of the harvest. And belongings and weapons.

Come with us Cai. There is nothing to fear.

CAI. Fear is it! (*CAI spits again.*)

PRIEST. We will go to Camulodunum, for the protection of the Government.

FIRST VILLAGER. Can't stand here arguing with you, Cai!

SECOND VILLAGER. Let the old fool stew.

THIRD VILLAGER. You want to see your daughters raped? And have the Saxons eat your brains, over a fire?

SECOND VILLAGER. Leave him behind. Gaga old bugger.

PRIEST. No no.

A silence.

Saxon raiders, Cai. After all these years of peace.

But you're an old fighter.

You know what an English raid means.

CAI. I am!
I am an old fighter of the Saxons. I don't need you — come and stand on my field to tell me that. Priest.

FIRST VILLAGER. We're wasting time. Let the old heathen be cut to bits. (*He turns to go.*)

SECOND VILLAGER (*going*). Can't wait any longer, old man! All the village, the women and children, out on the tracks in the woods already.

We don't go now we'll lose 'em —

PRIEST. In the name of pity, Cai!

CAI. Get off! Get off my field!

And you, Priest. With your cross of Jesus.

SECOND VILLAGER. That's it then.

He turns away. The other VILLAGERS *follow. They shout back as they go. The* PRIEST *stands still.*

FIRST VILLAGER. Ought to stone the bugger.

THIRD VILLAGER. We did right by you and yours, Cai. As neighbours.

PRIEST. Christ go with you.

CAI. Good riddance.

The PRIEST *hesitates, then goes off quickly after the* VILLAGERS. *Then* CAI *laughs.*

You're running the wrong way!

The Saxons will burn Camulodunum!

First thing to burn!

He laughs. Then is silent.

(*Aside*:) An old fighter of the Saxons. Here I sit, by the ruin of my field.

Me, veteran of Badon Hill.

When we cut the Saxons to bits. Once and for all. Smashed them back into their Kent marshes. Once and for all.

Huh.

As a soldier, how many commanders have I heard say, as a villager, how many times have I heard priests say — 'Once and for all.' Fight! Repent! Go on, on and on, once and for all!

After a life-time of it, I forgive myself.

I'll stay where I was born. And watch.

It all —

come —

again —

He lifts a wooden idol from the ground. He wipes the earth from it. He kisses it.

N.B. *During* CHICHESTER's *speech he stays on stage and carefully reburies the idol in the ground. At the end of* CHICHESTER's *speech he goes off.*

Scene Three

CHICHESTER *sits up suddenly.*

CHICHESTER. I'm soaking!

He stands up, brushing his clothes.

How is the intellectual at war?

Soaked with dew and pissed by eight in the morning.

He looks up.

Hot day. The banners will be bright. The horses, the shields and the swords.

He starts, looking at the trees.

God. Losing your marbles, old son.

With a parade ground manner.

Captain Thomas Chichester!

Yes Sir?

What are you doing?

Waiting to kill a man called O'Rourke, Sir!

Get on with it then!

Yes Sir!

Men have died with the training you've had, lad! So what is your problem?

No problem Sir!

He is out of breath. He waits.

Just one question Sir!

(*He breathes, then shouts again*:) When will peace come?

(*Then, low*:) When will peace come, Sir?

England out of Ireland? Swords into plough-shares, machine-guns to rakes, ammunition to fertilizer?

The dead in any war would vote for peace, Sir.

He breathes. Parade ground again.

You're a British Army Officer! Stop wanking! Put myself on a charge, Sir! Do that Captain! Thank you Sir!

He covers his face with his hands, he takes them away quickly.

He turns on his heel, eyeing the countryside.

He takes off his coat, puts it on the ground and lies on it. He lights a cigarette. He blows a cloud of smoke up.

(*He shouts:*) O'Rourke! Come on brother, le me blow your head off!

He sends another cloud of smoke up, as —

Scene Four

CORDA *and* MORGANA *run on on opposite sides of the stage. A* SAXON SOLDIER *crashes through the trees into the field. He is mortally wounded.*

SAXON. Feta gehwone. Ic eom gewundod: welc hearm maeg ic to the gedon?

He falls. The sisters watch him. He crawls a little way then stops.

MORGANA. What was he shouting?

CORDA. What do you think? At women.

MORGANA. His arm was jerking in a funny way.

Oh Corda, is he dead?

CORDA. Where's father?

MORGANA. Messing about.

CORDA. Get him.

MORGANA. But —

CORDA. Go and get our father! Go on!

MORGANA (*as she runs off along the edge of the field*). Oh he's got to be dead, oh Mary Mother of Jesus let him be dead.

MORGANA is off. A silence. Then the SAXON stands.

He and CORDA stare.

CORDA picks up a stone.

SAXON. Waelhreowan men! Is eower hete swa to anum eltheoditan geriht?

CORDA throws the stone. It misses him widely.

Wielisce wyrgen! Ic the on twa gescieran wille.

He stumbles a few paces towards her then falls. He drags himself a short distance.

Ic eom anhaga, iserne wund.

He grabs a sheaf, it falls about him.

A silence.

Then MORGANA comes on, pulling CAI by the hand.

CAI. Saxon in my field —

MORGANA. Come on, father — please —

CAI. The old stories, the old lies.

Plagues. Dragons. One-eyed giants eating girls.

CORDA. Look!

Just look at what's wandered into your field!

Turning away.

My poor old, stumbling, brutal father.

CAI. Damage to crops? Wild boar, chasing field mice.

Bah! When wild animals come out and fool in your fields, what is that? When there's nothing to keep 'em down, what is that?

The ruin of Britain.

The SAXON groans and shifts in the sheaf. They all see the movement. They are still.

Then CAI strides to the SAXON, takes his sword and kills him.

MORGANA *prays, weeping.*

MORGANA. Oh love of Christ our Lord. Oh love of the Mother of Christ our Lord, gentle Mary.

CORDA. Now we know there is a war.

Now we know there is a war.

Now we've got to run away.

CAI. Shut your mouth, girl.

CORDA. Don't you even see what you've just killed? Are you that far gone? Gaga old fool.

CAI. Give you a beating girl!

MORGANA (*to* CORDA). Please, don't —

CORDA. A Saxon Soldier.

Look.

That dead thing. Pagan thing.

MORGANA. The Priest said the Saxons believe God is a giant. Who smashes children's heads with a hammer.

CORDA. Don't be stupid, Morgana.

MORGANA. Oh and you're so clever, just 'cos you want to go to a townhouse. And a steward gave you a town dress which father made you burn —

CORDA. Shut up!

CAI. Peace!

CAI *clenches the sword.*

CORDA. We must go!

CAI. Peace!

CORDA. There'll be more of them!

A silence.

Father!

CAI. Twenty-one years of peace. And the killing when I was a boy, forgotten. The Saxons from the South, the Irish from the West, only stories and lies, told by monks on the road out for alms. Poets in winter, out for a good meal. And powerful men, only rumours. Bandits calling themselves 'Emperors', 'New Romans'.

Twenty-one years. A kind of peace, on the same fields, under the same skies.

He gestures at the SAXON.

We'll bury that. Harvest our fields.

CORDA. We'll die.

CAI. That one was alone. Legs torn to bits. Been stumbling about in the forest. Lost his troop.

Dunno. What's it to me?

He begins to dig with the sword at the edge of the field.

CORDA. I'll go with Morgana.

CAI. Do that and my curse goes with you.

CORDA. Better cursed than dead.

CAI. You'll be a leper, girl.

He digs again.

Like all the others. On the roads, in the ditches.
He stops digging.

I remember it. Families on the roads. Following my mother's skirt. Her feet clay and blood.

He digs again, angrily.

Running from the Saxons. Huh!

MORGANA. We'll be all right, Corda! I'll put up a little shrine by the field. To the cross of our Mother of Christ —

CORDA *kneels.*

CORDA. I kneel in front of you like a daughter asking for your blessing, to be married.

CAI. Out of my way.

MORGANA. What are you digging?

CAI. She sleeps here.

CORDA. But I don't want to be married. Just to stay alive.

CAI. Get back!

He lifts a blackened wooden idol from the earth.

MORGANA. What —

CAI. Goddess of this place, girl.

MORGANA. A saint? It's not a saint.

CAI. Huh! Why didn't you die when you were born?

Both of you, eh?

Why didn't all of us die of your mother's sickness?

Touching the idol, gently.

Because of the blood put on the ground where I buried her.
Twenty-one years ago.

MORGANA. Filthy! A filthy pagan thing —

CAI. Right girl. She's not like your skinny rabbit Jesus, nailed
up, soaking up prayers. This one don't soak up prayers.

He laughs, then stops.

(*Low:*) Get a little bowl. For blood from the Saxon's
throat.

MORGANA. No —

CAI. She'll see none of his kind come to this place again.

*CORDA and MORGANA hear something. CAI does not,
absorbed by the idol.*

CORDA. What did you hear?

MORGANA. Don't know. A woman cried.

CAI (*to CORDA*). You girl! Get a rope and a knife.

CORDA picks up a stone. She and CAI stare at each other.

CAI. Ah. Ah.

Kind against kind.

The cow gives birth to wolves who tear her belly to bits.

Ah.

*CORDA brings the stone down on CAI's head. He goes on
all fours, staring at her.*

Then he stands and staggers away.

MORGANA. Corda.

Don't.

*She tries to hold CORDA back. CORDA pushes her away.
She holds CORDA about her knees.*

*CORDA kicks her away. She turns and runs after CAI.
They disappear into the trees.*

Saint Pelagius said we're not born into the world evil. We
make our own sin.

Corda! Please! We've not murdered our own father, on our own field!

(*To herself:*) Yes, we make our own sin. The Priest said they call that a heresy and they sent a Bishop from Rome, with soldiers to make us learn —

CORDA *comes out of the trees, the stone still in her hand and bloody.*

She stops a distance from MORGANA.

Learn — that we're born in sin. Even in the cradle, bad. Filthy.

Please, we're not murderers —

CORDA, *moving quickly to where the idol lies on the ground.*

CORDA. He's got some old coins, buried. Maybe by this thing —

MORGANA. He must have a mass, with a priest. Or he'll not go to Heaven —

CORDA *throws the idol to one side. She starts to dig with the sword.*

CORDA. Come on. Help me!

MORGANA. If we drag him into the field, they'll think he was killed by the Saxon —

CORDA. What an evil thought, sister.

MORGANA. I loved him.

CORDA. I hated him. Ever since he lifted my skirt when I was only just a woman.

He did the same to you.

MORGANA. No.

CORDA. Don't lie.

MORGANA. I've only seen the village. All my life, never out of sight.

What's out there? Dragons? Giants?

Is there a war out there?

CORDA *lifts a handful of coins.*

CORDA. I've found them. They're shiny. They're gold. Hurry up, take yours.

MORGANA. No.

A silence.

CORDA. You're right. We don't know anything.

Has there been a battle with the Saxons? We don't know. Are the towns burning? We don't know.

Sickness travels in the air. Whatever it is out there, the war — travels in the air. We're breathing it. It makes a daughter kill her father and rob him. Just like that.

If you won't come I'll kill you too.

In the far distance a woman's voice screams.

MORGANA. I heard it again.

CORDA. Get up to the little wood. Along the ditches.

CORDA, *holding the money in her skirt, scampers away.*
MORGANA *hesitates and crosses herself, looking at the idol.*

Come on little sister.

They run off.

Scene Five

CHICHESTER *asleep. The light changes to a sunlit, late afternoon.*
An IRISH WOMAN *comes on.*

WOMAN. You.

CHICHESTER *wakes with a start. A silence. Then he stands, hurriedly. He speaks in upper-class English.*

CHICHESTER. Where's O'Rourke?

WOMAN. The British Army was here.

CHICHESTER. I didn't see them. What did the bastards want?

A silence.

WOMAN. What's your name?

CHICHESTER. O'Rourke knows my name.

A silence.

My name is Henwick. Lliam Henwick.

WOMAN. You've been putting it about you're an Irishman, Mr Henwick.

CHICHESTER. Of Anglo-Irish parentage. My family's house was burnt down in 1918 because my grandfather, something of a romantic drunk, went over to the Republican cause.

But you will have telephoned the backwater in County-Limerick that gave my father breath.

Don't piss me about love.

WOMAN. You have a token of your good faith.

CHICHESTER. For O'Rourke.

The WOMAN, impassive.

All right!

He takes out the pistol. He hands it to her. She examines it.

I'm a friend of the Republican cause.

And a businessman.

The WOMAN turns and walks away, taking the pistol.

Tell O'Rourke to come today!

The Republican cause is just!

Trust me! It's in my blood! The great wrong of England in Ireland!

The WOMAN has gone.

(*To himself:*) Believe it, don't you Tom. In a way, Tom.

I am the great wrong in Ireland.

He retches.

The fear worse than you thought, Tom?

He wipes his mouth.

But then a trained assassin is bound to be a dangerous man with dangerous thoughts.

He laughs.

In the distance, a woman's voice screams.

He goes to the edge of the field. He takes out another pistol from a hiding place. He puts it in his clothing.

A woman's voice screams again.

CHICHESTER *lies down and closes his eyes. He flicks at a fly.*

Bugger off. Bugger off, Celtic fly.

He falls asleep.

Scene Six

CHICHESTER *turns over on his side, fast asleep, stretching an arm up.*

CHICHESTER. Ah!

His arm falls. He settles in his sleep.

The WOMAN's *voice screaming, nearer.*

Again, the voice even nearer.

Then two COOKS, *both young, the* FIRST *fat and the* SECOND *thin, carry* ADONA *on an improvised stretcher. Her face is hidden by veils of silk, her body covered by richly embroidered and coloured cloths. A* STEWARD, *a fit, capable man, walks by the side of the stretcher.*

When ADONA *speaks, the silks of her veils flutter.*

ADONA. Don't bump me!

FIRST COOK. My back's gone!

STEWARD. Watch the crops! I won't have crops kicked about! Even in this godforsaken —

FIRST COOK. But it's my back, it's gone.

SECOND COOK. His back's gone.

FIRST COOK. Oh!

The FIRST COOK *falls to his knees. The stretcher lurches.*

ADONA. What are you doing!

STEWARD. Put her down.

ADONA. Don't you care? Don't you have any respect?

FIRST COOK. Sorry.

STEWARD. Gently!

The STEWARD helps them put the stretcher down.

Shit.

*The three men squat, exhausted. They look at the sheaves
then at each other. They each stand and rush to a sheaf. They
rub ears of wheat between their hands blowing the chaff
away. They eat desperately, throughout the scene.*

SECOND COOK. First field for miles, not harvested or burnt.
We could bake bread! Stone bread — last us for days —

ADONA. Steward! Up again!

STEWARD. My Lady —

ADONA. Where I am — the household is! The house may be
burnt! But the household is here!

The man who fell down! Whip him!

FIRST COOK. I'm just a cook Madam, who worked in your
kitchens!

ADONA. Whip him. Where I can see.

STEWARD (*to himself*). Shit.

SECOND COOK. That's right Ma'am. We know about feeding
you, not carrying you about.

STEWARD. We have to rest my lady, if we're going to stay
alive.

ADONA. You're going to abandon me.

The STEWARD shouts.

STEWARD. No!

ADONA. You'll all be punished. Do you hear? When things are
put to rights. When the Legions come from Rome.

SECOND COOK. She goes on and on about Romans coming to
save her.

I don't believe there ever were Romans.

Or the children's story is right. The Romans were giant,
stone snails. The roads are the slime they left behind.

FIRST COOK. I've seen the recipes of Ancient Rome. They were real enough. Bastards with bellies lined with iron.

The FIRST COOK *winces and holds his back.*

SECOND COOK. Your back bad?

FIRST COOK. Nothing wrong with it. I'm going to talk to this bastard.

The FIRST COOK *winks. The* SECOND COOK *touches his nose. The* SECOND COOK *begins to wander away, eating ears of wheat. The* STEWARD *is hunched.*

(*To the* STEWARD:) A powerful lady, our Mistress.

STEWARD. Indeed.

FIRST COOK. Three days lugging her about. What she got under there?

SECOND COOK. Must be wine. She's pissed.

STEWARD. Huh.

SECOND COOK. Smells like she's shat herself.

STEWARD. That's enough.

A silence.

The SECOND COOK *moves further away.*

FIRST COOK. I say run. Leave the old bag.

STEWARD. I didn't hear that.

The STEWARD *grabs the* FIRST COOK *by the throat.*

FIRST COOK. I just want to get on with my trade.

STEWARD. Cooking?

The STEWARD *scoffs and pushes him away.*

FIRST COOK. My family goes back a long way. To the kitchens of the Emperors of Rome.
There's a story in my family. One of us, a long time ago, served up an ox to an Emperor. Whole. 'What?' cried the Emperor. 'Cook an ox with the entrails and all the shit entire?' And my ancestor is dragged in on his knees. He begs a sword. But not for his throat. He slashes the ox's basted belly — and out tumble, why chicken hearts, stewed larks, the tasty livers of little lambs. The kidneys of the ox drained of the blood and folded in the delicate flesh of marinated,

white fish. All of it bound with butter, garlic, parsley and dry white wine.

The Imperial Ox! I've always wanted to cook it.

The trick is that with all that offal you don't need salt in the stuffing.

STEWARD. Huh. Things being what they are you're going to be out of a job.

FIRST COOK. Yeah, I wonder what they're all eating out there, these days.

S'pose I can go and cook for the Saxons. Human brains. Tricky, brain dishes.

STEWARD. Where did you hear the Saxons are cannibals?

FIRST COOK. Aren't they?

STEWARD. They're dirt farmers. Just like us.

FIRST COOK. Be better to kill her. Kinder.

You know we're going to have to.

STEWARD. I am her lover.

FIRST COOK. Oh?

A silence.

Nice work?

STEWARD. Lords, ladies, masters, workers in the fields — cooks — what do you all want of me?

I breathe my first breath. Look up. I am the son of a tin miner. A godforsaken trade on this good, sweet earth.

But as the priests say — 'The world, cold thing, is a sermon.'

I get education from the priests. I get out of the Cornish mines by selling myself as a bondsman.

I please a master by doing a murder. I am released from my bondsmanship.

I learn. Gain dignity. I become, in early middle-life, a steward to a great estate.

I carry the estate in my head, in my dreams. Seed-times. Debts. Tallies. Who's sick, who's stupid, who can be relied on.

Like a huge riddle that only I can answer.

And when the mistress of the estate, of the riddle, wants me in her bed, do I go?

Do I. Like a rat down a hole.

Cook, you run off, I will find you. When the raids have stopped. And I am back in my lady's bed. I will manacle you to a wall and, with great pleasure, drive a nail through your tongue.

FIRST COOK. Yeah. Well. We'll see.

STEWARD. You will.

The SECOND COOK *finds the dead* SAXON.

SECOND COOK. Oh no. I'm standing here looking at a corpse. And I think it's Saxon.

The STEWARD *and the* FIRST COOK *look at each other.*

And I'm going to be sick.

FIRST COOK. He's going to be sick.

STEWARD. You two are the lowest of the low.

FIRST COOK. Dunno. When you come down to it, I'm meat and he's vegetables.

The SECOND COOK *is sick.*

STEWARD. Oh dear oh dear.

The STEWARD *walks over to the* SAXON.

ADONA. Steward, what are you doing? Steward!

John!

SECOND COOK. Bad habit for a cook, throwing up all the time. And I think I'm going to see one or two corpses in the days ahead.

ADONA. John. I'm hurting.

STEWARD. They've gone further North than we thought.

He kicks the SAXON *and turns away.*

We'll leave, now.

SECOND COOK. How about threshing this lot —

STEWARD. Too dangerous.

ADONA. You're going to kill me and leave me in a ditch. I'm getting up!

STEWARD. No, My Lady —

He runs to her.

ADONA. You won't whip them? I will!

FIRST COOK. Run for it.

SECOND COOK. He'll kill us —

FIRST COOK. Come on!

SECOND COOK. We won't work in better kitchens than hers —

FIRST COOK. By now our lovely kitchens are gone up in
flames — her great house with it —

ADONA. Where is the whip?

STEWARD. I beg you my love —

ADONA *stands. She throws her veils back. She is disfigured
by plague.*

A silence.

SECOND COOK. Help me. What's she got?

Someone, what's she got? Oh help me, please.

The SECOND COOK *vomits.*

ADONA. Yellow plague.

What do you expect when civilisation dies? Good health?

STEWARD. Stay in her service.

That's your best chance.
Carry around someone with that, no one will dare come
near you.

And come the winter — the fields empty — no crops for the
English to scavenge for their troops — it'll all stop.

Powerful men will drink themselves back into some kind of
Government, through the winter.

The great houses will be rebuilt. Kitchens with big ovens.

I beg you, don't leave us! It's only a disease! It can only kill
you!

FIRST COOK (*low*). On the whole, is the world falling apart?

SECOND COOK (*low*). On the whole, yes.

FIRST COOK (*low*). Run up to that little wood.

SECOND COOK (*low*). Right.

STEWARD. If you won't help us out of fear, how about pity?

ADONA. Whip them! Chain them!

> (*To the* COOKS:) You're staring at a Roman matron.

> Restore the Empire! Rebuild the towns. Appoint magistrates. Drive the raiders back. Set up gibbets in the fields to punish deserters.

FIRST COOK. Lady, the Romans left Britain a hundred years ago.

ADONA. Whip him! I am a Roman.

SECOND COOK. There weren't any Romans. And if there were, they're all dead.

> *A silence.*

ADONA. The slave's right.

> We are ghosts. Roman standards lie rotting on the ground. We stoop to pick them up. Our hands pass through them, like smoke.

FIRST COOK (*to the* SECOND COOK). Run.

> *The* COOKS *run off.*

ADONA. Now you have no one to carry me.

STEWARD. No.

> *They stare at each other.*

ADONA. Rob me then.

STEWARD. I have to, my Lady.

> *He goes to the stretcher. He takes three small sacks from beneath the covers.*

ADONA. Like a dog.

> No, not a dog. A dog would sniff around my grave. Whine for me.

> *The* STEWARD *takes out a knife.*

ADONA. I was a great lady. I took you into my bed. You were my pleasure, my fields were my pleasure, my gardens, my harvests, the roofs of my house in the sun, my place in a civilised world.

STEWARD. Now you're a refugee too. With runny bowels and a dangerous disease.

She tries to run, falls and crawls. He takes her by the shoulder and puts the knife into the back of her neck.

She screams, then is silent.

What kind of animal am I?

A survivor.

I was a bondsman. I was a servant. I was a prostitute.

Goodbye my dead Lady, goodbye my dead masters. Now I'm free of you.

Thank God war has come.

He walks away quickly into the trees, the three bags on his shoulders.

Scene Seven

The light changes. A sunset. Golden yellow light, O'ROURKE walks out of the trees. CHICHESTER opens his eyes, sees him and sits up.

O'ROURKE. Good evening to you.

Two MEN with automatic weapons come out of the trees. The WOMAN walks quickly across.

So you're a friend of the Republican cause, Mr Henwick.

CHICHESTER *stands. A silence.*

You're a strange and puzzling man to us, Mr Henwick. Here you are on an Irish farm, out of the goodness of your heart helping a bedridden old woman, her sons being scattered by British economic imperialism. You are heard singing in the pubs. Spreading it about that you are no friend of the British Government. Then sending us messages that you are a gun-runner, with communist weapons for sale.

Now as I see it, you're either a madman, or an intelligence officer with the Special Air Services Regiment.

One way or the other.

So you'd better convince me quick that you're stone crazy.

See if he's armed.

The two armed MEN *advance on* CHICHESTER.

CHICHESTER. I am —

I am a British Officer.

The two MEN *stop dead still.*

A long silence.

My name is Thomas Edward Chichester.

Henwick was my cover.

I come from an old English Army family. My father was killed by a landmine in Cyprus, when I was a baby.

My mission was to assassinate you, O'Rourke.

A silence, then:

O'ROURKE (*slowly*). Now why, in God's name, do you tell me that?

A silence.

FIRST MAN. Kill the bastard.

O'ROURKE. Be quiet.

SECOND MAN. This could be a set-up —

O'ROURKE. I don't think so. What is your rank?

CHICHESTER. Captain.

O'ROURKE. You have just spoken your death warrant, Captain Chichester.

Why?

CHICHESTER. I keep on seeing the dead. A field in Ireland, a field in England. And faces like wood. Charred wood, set in the ground. Staring at me.

The faces of our forefathers.

Their eyes are sockets of rain-water, flickering with gnats. They stare at me in terror.

Because in my hand there's a Roman spear. A Saxon axe. A British Army machine-gun.

The weapons of Rome, invaders, Empire.

O'ROURKE. This is one hell of a way to deny your Imperial heritage. That what you're trying to do, Captain?

CHICHESTER, *gripping the wrist of his right hand, shaking it.*

CHICHESTER. The weapons. I want to throw them down.

And reach down. To the faces. Hold the burnt heads in my hands and pull them up. The bodies out of the earth. Hold them against me.

Their bones of peat and water and mud. And work them back to life.

Like King Arthur —

FIRST MAN. Christ Almighty! He's raving mad.

He laughs.

SECOND MAN. Let's have done with him.

O'ROURKE. I think he may just be an honourable man, having a hard time of it. The assassin, humanised by his trade.

O'ROURKE *laughs.*

Is that it Captain? The horrors of war?

WOMAN. What right does he have to stand in a field in Ireland and talk of the horrors of war? What nation ever learnt from the sufferings it inflicted on others? What did the Roman Empire give to the people it enslaved? Concrete. What did the British Empire give to its colonies? Tribal wars. I don't want to hear of this British soldier's humanity. And how he comes to be howling in the middle of my country. And how he thinks Ireland is a tragedy. Ireland's troubles are not a tragedy. They are the crimes his country has done mine. That he does to me, by standing there.

O'ROURKE (*to the two* MEN). When you've disarmed him, shoot him.

A silence. CHICHESTER *begins to tremble.*

CHICHESTER. You murdering bastards —

The SECOND MAN *shoots him.*

CHICHESTER *fumbles for his gun.*

When will peace come? When will peace come? When will peace come?

The SECOND MAN *shoots him again.*

O'ROURKE. Ah Moraed. What will we do when we have peace?

WOMAN. Peace will take care of itself. War will not.

The THREE MEN, O'ROURKE *and the* WOMAN *walk away.*

A moon shines, the light goes as —

Scene Eight

Brilliant moonlight. CORDA *and* MORGANA *creep into the trees.* CORDA *still carries the* ENGLISHMAN's *sword.*

MORGANA. Father's not here! He's still alive!

CORDA. No. Here he is. Touch him.

MORGANA. No.

CORDA. We came back so you could. Touch him.

MORGANA *touches* CAI's *hand.*

MORGANA. Oh.

CORDA. We'll get his clothes off.

MORGANA. Why do that?

CORDA. Men's clothes. We can sell them.

MORGANA. I can't.

CORDA. Sister, we're beggars now. This is how we'll live.

MORGANA. Oh why aren't there fires in the village? Why aren't the cattle mooing and coughing? Why aren't husbands and wives laughing or rowing at their evening meal?

CORDA. Help me.

Then we'll rob the dead Saxon. Come on.

The two COOKS *come on.* MORGANA *sees them.*

MORGANA. Corda —

CORDA. What?

Sh.

CORDA *and* MORGANA *hide.*

SECOND COOK. Why do we have to come back down here —

FIRST COOK. We saw him kill the old bag. Maybe he left something.

SECOND. So quiet. Could be a trap!

FIRST COOK. Why are Saxon Soldiers going to set a trap for a Second Cook?

SECOND COOK. This field. Standing among corpses. Their ghosts will be out.

FIRST COOK. There she is!

The FIRST COOK *goes to the dead* ADONA. *He throws the coverings from the stretcher about.*

Nothing but cushions.

SECOND COOK. That smell.

Oh, it's her. I can't be sick anymore. I have given my all.

He sees CORDA *and* MORGANA.

Now I'm seeing the ghosts.

FIRST COOK. For fucksake.

The FIRST COOK *sees* CORDA *and* MORGANA.

CORDA. We're women with Saxon Soldiers. You touch us, they'll cut your bollocks off.

SECOND COOK. Yeah, well actually we're cooks.

MORGANA. Cooks?

CORDA. Have you got food?

SECOND COOK. You give us food and we'll cook it.

MORGANA. We've not got any food.

SECOND COOK. Goodbye then.

FIRST COOK. No wait, wait.

Where are the soldiers you're with then?

MORGANA. Don't you try and touch us. We're sisters — we killed our father —

FIRST COOK. Oh really?

CORDA. Oh really. We've got a Saxon sword.

She raises the sword.

MORGANA. And we don't care! We've killed once so we're going to hell anyway.

FIRST COOK. So he's dead. Your father.

A silence.

Our Mistress is dead too.

SECOND COOK. He's right! That was her! Don't you think her smell's like a little cloud — over everything?

FIRST COOK. Shut up.

(*To* CORDA *and* MORGANA:) So what you going to do?

MORGANA. What's that to you?

CORDA. Go on the road. Get away. Kill the Saxons.

SECOND COOK. Oh aye —

FIRST COOK. Look — now don't wave that about. And don't run off. But maybe we'd better stay together for a bit — be a bit of an Army.

CORDA *laughs.*

CORDA. An army of cooks? What use are cooks now?

SECOND COOK. That had crossed our minds.

MORGANA. They're dangerous men —

SECOND COOK. We're not dangerous. Utterly fucked, actually.

CORDA. So what can you be?

FIRST COOK. What can you be?

CORDA. A mother of killers, Cook. Children brought up right. Like stoats, like weasels, like otters.

A cook's not going to be much good for that.

FIRST COOK. I'm changing my trade.

CORDA. To what?

FIRST COOK. Poet.

SECOND COOK. What are you talking about? You can't even read —

FIRST COOK. Shut up. We're on here —

MORGANA. What do we want with them, Corda?

CORDA. We're going to have to travel a long way. We need all the men and women we can find.

What poem you got then? In your new trade.

FIRST COOK. 'Bout a King!

A silence.

CORDA. Yes?

FIRST COOK. King.

Not any King.

CORDA. No?

FIRST COOK. No.

CORDA. Did he have a Queen, this King?

SECOND COOK. Yes.

He hesitates.

Yes, oh very sexy —

FIRST COOK. Look let me do the meat, right?

SECOND COOK. Oh yeah, I do the vegetables even when it comes to fucking poetry.

FIRST COOK. Actually, he was a King who never was.

His Government was the people of Britain. His peace was as common as rain or sun. His law was as natural as grass, growing in a meadow.

And there never was a Government, or a peace, or a law like that.

His sister murdered his father. His wife was unfaithful. He died by the treachery of his best friend.

And when he was dead, the King who never was and the Government that never was — were mourned. And remembered. Bitterly.

And thought of as a golden age, lost and yet to come.

CORDA. Very pretty.

MORGANA. What was his name?

FIRST COOK. Any old name dear. (*To the* SECOND COOK:) What was his name?

SECOND COOK. Right. Er — any old name.
    Arthur?
    Arthur?

Further titles in the Methuen Modern Plays series are described on the following pages.

Methuen's Modern Plays

Jean Anouilh	*Antigone*
	Becket
	The Lark
	Ring Round the Moon
John Arden	*Serjeant Musgrave's Dance*
	The Workhouse Donkey
	Armstrong's Last Goodnight
	Pearl
John Arden and	*The Royal Pardon*
Margaretta D'Arcy	*The Hero Rises Up*
	The Island of the Mighty
	Vandaleur's Folly
Wolfgang Bauer	*Shakespeare the Sadist*
Rainer Werner	
Fassbinder	*Bremen Coffee*
Peter Handke	*My Foot My Tutor*
Franz Xaver Kroetz	*Stallerhof*
Brendan Behan	*The Quare Fellow*
	The Hostage
	Richard's Cork Leg
Edward Bond	*A-A-America!* and *Stone*
	Saved
	Narrow Road to the Deep North
	The Pope's Wedding
	Lear
	The Sea
	Bingo
	The Fool and *We Come to the River*
	Theatre Poems and Songs
	The Bundle
	The Woman
	The Worlds with *The Activists Papers*
	Restoration and *The Cat*
	Summer and *Fables*

Peter Whelan   *The Accrington Pals*
Nigel Williams   *Line 'Em*
                    Class Enemy
Victoria Wood   *Good Fun and Talent*
Theatre Workshop   *Oh What a Lovely War*